4 TRIBES 1 EARTH

A Parable of Communication and Love

PIP McKAY

Published by
UNICORN PRESS
THE MAGIC OF TRANSFORMATION

Copyright © Pip McKay 2017
First Edition Jan 2011
Second Edition 2018

This book is copyright. Apart from any fair dealing for the purposes of private study research, criticism or review, as permitted under the Australian Copyright Act 1968, no part may be reproduced by any process without written permission from the author. Every effort has been made to provide accurate and authoritative information in this book. Neither the publisher or the author accepts any liability for injury, loss or damage caused to any person acting as a result of information in this book nor for any errors or omissions. Readers are advised that this book is not meant to replace or be instead of any counseling, psychology or psychiatric advice and if a reader needs this support to obtain advise from a licensed professional before acting on information provided in this book.

Book Cover Design: Kylie Maxwell, ePrintDesign
Internal Design: Kylie Maxwell, ePrintDesign
Avatar Character Drawings and their Habitat: Pavel Kosgolov, Delorean
ISBN: 9780994446732

To my beloved mother, Elaine and my partner Will, for all their support and understanding.

CONTENTS

About Pip McKay... 6
Forward by Michelle Duval.. 8
Introduction by Pip McKay... 10

SECTION 1 — 4 TRIBES 1 EARTH   19
Act 1   23
Act 1, Scene 1   Wind-In-Her-Hair From The Tribe-That-Moves-And-Is-Touched .. 24
Act 1, Scene 2   Bright-Eagle – The Girl Who Feels Too Much 27
Act 1, Scene 3   Wind-In-Her-Hair – The Cave Of Feeling 31
Act 1, Scene 4   Bright-Eagle – The Girl Who Touched Me 33
Act 1, Scene 5   Wind-In-Her-Hair – The Chase Begins 34
Act 1, Scene 6   Bright-Eagle Sees His Father 35
Act 1, Scene 7   Wind-In-Her-Hair Connects With The Story Of Her Parents 38

Act 2   39
Act 2, Scene 1   Bear-Heart, Speaks – He Hears The Song................. 40
Act 2, Scene 2   Bird-Song Speaks – She Feels The Song 43
Act 2, Scene 3   Bird-Song Is Hit By The Arrow 45
Act 2, Scene 4   Bear-Heart's Heart Echoes 48
Act 2, Scene 5   Bird-Song Hears The Pounding Call....................... 50
Act 2, Scene 6   Bear-Heart Silences The Thunder 53
Act 2, Scene 7   Bird-Song Squashes The Call............................. 55
Act 2, Scene 8   Bear-Heart Sings The Approach........................... 57
Act 2, Scene 9   Bird-Song Calls To Her Father's Spirit.................. 59
Act 2, Scene 10 Bear-Heart Listens To His Heart's Desire................ 61
Act 2, Scene 11 Bird-Song's Heart Cries................................. 63
Act 2, Scene 12 Wind-In-Her-Hair Completes The Story.................... 67
Act 2, Scene 13 Bright-Eagle Wants His Bride............................ 69

Act 3   73
Act 3, Scene 1   Andrew From The Tribe-That-Thinks-And-Calculates........ 74
Act 3, Scene 2   Javier Translates 77
Act 3, Scene 3   Andrew Meets The Tribe.................................. 79

Act 3, Scene 4	Javier Sees The Sun	81
Act 3, Scene 5	Andrew Begins To See	83
Act 3, Scene 6	Javier And The Brittle Forest	85
Act 3, Scene 7	Andrew Starts To Feel	87
Act 3, Scene 8	Javier Feels The Heartbeat Of The Forest Fade	89
Act 3, Scene 9	Andrew Overflows	91
Act 3, Scene 10	Javier And The Wedding	95
Act 3, Scene 11	Andrew Learns To Speak From The Heart	98
Act 3, Scene 12	Javier And His Little Sister Jenny	103
Act 3, Scene 13	Andrew Observes Javier And The Tribes	105
Act 3, Scene 14	Javier Translates For Andrew At The Gathering	110
Act 3, Scene 15	Andrew Listens To Jenny	116
Act 3, Scene 16	Javier Begins To Open His Heart To His Little Sister	122
Act 3, Scene 17	Andrew And Jenny Fall In Love	125
Epilogue	Jenny Speaks About Their Shared Dream	135

SECTION 2 — THE DIFFERENT TRIBES   133

General Introduction To The Tribes 135
Tribe-That-Sees-And-Has-Visions 137
Tribe-That-Moves-And-Is-Touched 141
Tribe-That-Listens-And-Sings 147
Tribe-That-Thinks-And-Calculates 152
Conclusion 158

SECTION 3 — UNDERSTANDING THE THEORY BEHIND COMMUNICATION STYLES AND HOW THE TRIBES CAME ABOUT   159

General Introduction To Communication Styles 162
Why Are The Tribes Different? 165
Where Did The Idea Of Communication Styles Come From? 167
Pip McKay's Learning Journey 170

ABOUT

Pip McKay

Pip McKay is a highly respected thought leader and pioneer within the field of personal transformation, coaching and NLP. She is also an Amazon Number 1, award winning author for her book, *The 8 Principles of Achievement, Love and Happiness*.

She has dedicated over 20 years of her life to creating techniques which allow you to discover your unique passion and purpose, remove negative influences, fulfil your true potential and communicate effectively.

When Pip was young she was diagnosed with dyslexia and ADHD. She also suffered from depression and chronic fatigue. Pip overcame these issues to gain a BA Honours degree in English Literature and a Diploma of Education with Distinction from The University of Sydney, where she won the P.R. Cole Memorial Prize for Excellence.

Pip taught in England and was a GCSE examiner then returned home to teach acting at The McDonald College of Performing Arts and was chosen as an HSC examiner. Pip ran the education arm of the Sydney Theatre Company before creating her own acting company, Spark Productions. She was then headhunted to be the Corporate Director of Accelerated Learning Worldwide.

During her years as a teacher, trainer and director, Pip found that she was naturally coaching students and staff, dealing with issues ranging from performance and confidence enhancement through to cases of trauma and abuse. This prompted her to study Neuro-Linguistic Programming (NLP) to enhance her skills. Pip became a recognised trainer of NLP and cofounded the Australian Board of NLP. She combined NLP with her experience as a teacher to create products such as *Kid's Matrix, Focus on Kids DVDs* and now *4 Tribes 1 Earth*.

Pip pioneered the entire field of *Matrix Therapies*® and *Archetypal Coaching*®. Her proven techniques have been taught throughout Australia and internationally, including most recently Israel. Through her company *Evolve Now!*

Mind Institute, Pip has assisted thousands of people to learn, transform and grow.

Just hearing Pip speak is transformational – attending training or coaching sessions is life changing. Pip lives in Manly with her adored partner Will. She loves animals, nature and the beach.

To contact her or gain more information go to www.pipmckay.com.au

FOREWORD

Michelle Duval — Founder of *Fingerprint for Success*,
CEO of *Equilibrio* and best-selling author

There are only a handful of moments in life when you wish the world had stood still and a trumpet player with a bright red jacket arrived and trumpeted ceremoniously so you recognise your world will never be the same again.

I am wearing that bright red jacket. This is one of those moments. In this exquisitely crafted parable, Pip McKay opens your heart and mind to transcend difference and embrace communication and love with deep profundity.

I first had the joy of meeting Pip in the American Summer of 2000 in California. We were passionate students working closely together studying the world's greatest change agents in family therapy, cognitive science and neuro-linguistic programming (NLP).

I remember sitting in awe as I first witnessed Pip teach our group. She brought to life complex human systems with incredible simplicity that touched and inspired each of us in our diverse group of nationalities, stages of life, education and confidence.

I knew way back then that I was witnessing both a master and an alchemist. Rather than inspiration alone, we learnt from Pip real skills that could be used immediately in our daily lives and have remained pivotal for me today.

Unsurprised, but inspired all the same, I have enjoyed watching Pip quickly become one of the world's most respected change agents and also developers in cognitive science, coaching and NLP. The methodologies and processes that Pip has pioneered are used by therapists, coaches, consultants, teachers and parents all over the world, for genuine transformation and lasting change.

As an author, researcher and professional coach myself, I have had the privilege of working with some of the world's most successful actors, writers, producers, inventors, thought leaders and entrepreneurs. I have been invited to know them at an intimate level and support them through significant life, creative and commercial goals.

As a result of the vast number of people that I have worked with globally for over 20 years, I remain struck by the fact that those who have experienced the most success, joy and contentment in life, have an insatiable hunger for ongoing learning. They yearn to understand themselves and those around them at a very profound level.

This is what Pip invites you to do in this truly beautiful parable. She takes you on your own learning, personal and transformational adventure. Through the delightful, provocative and endearing characters of *4 Tribes 1 Earth*, you too gain access to this potent knowledge and understanding. She shows you how the characters, and therefore the reader, can transcend difference, conflict and difficulty to be able to empathise, connect, communicate and learn.

Using her playful trademark style, Pip has decoded and simplified the most impactful learning and communication principles and embedded them in the parable. Then for more conscious learning, at the back of the book she has outlined how these skills can be applied with children, relationships, teams and business.

To say that these skills underpin almost all aspects of wellbeing and success would be an understatement. No matter where you are in your pursuit to be, do and achieve all you can, *4 Tribes 1 Earth* will facilitate a meaningful and impactful shift within yourself, your relationships and your life.

Beyond significant personal impact, your embodiment of these life learnings will contribute to evolving how you learn from and communicate with others.

THANK YOU Pip for sharing your diverse talents, extensive wisdom and your deep and genuine empathy with humanity in this beautiful parable and its companions.

In doing so, you have made it possible for each person to use their unique mission, talents and skills for personal success and contribute to a far more peaceful, genuinely empathetic and connected world.

On behalf of our tribe of humanity, I say: "For this we are truly grateful".

INTRODUCTION

Pip McKay

I was one of those children who was totally disorganised. I never had the right books and couldn't get myself sorted in the morning. I remember one morning being so tired I put my uniform over the top of my shorty pyjamas and didn't even realise until I changed for sport!

I didn't do my homework either, mainly because I couldn't remember what it was. My homework diary was forgotten the moment I left the classroom. I never opened it at home.

What seemed normal to other children was a mystery to me but I didn't mind because I inhabited a magical world that happened each and every moment. I couldn't read, write or spell properly. I reversed my letters, couldn't even spell phonetically and had trouble recalling instructions. It didn't matter to me, in fact I didn't even notice, because the Narnia and Enid Blyton books that had been read to me as a child inhabited my waking moments and inspired all my games.

By the time I went to high school, I had some strategies in place. I made friends easily and would just follow along with them to find my classroom, borrow their pens, share their books and asked them about homework. When I look back at it now, I am amazed they put up with me! I also realised that if I liked a teacher, I could learn but if I didn't feel a connection, I was totally lost.

In Year 9 I was very lucky to have a breakthrough. I went to boarding school. We had to sit in the library in silence for two hours each school night. I was so bored and restless I opened up my homework diary. Low and behold there was all the homework written down and its due date! I know it seems incredible but I had never made the link between what I had written down for homework in the classroom and opening up the diary and seeing what I needed to do at home.

There was even a timetable showing all our classes, the rooms and the teachers. I noticed that a friend of mine had colour coded the timetable. Green for all the English classes, red for maths and so on. I decided to do the same and suddenly I could see a pattern. It was like a fog had been lifted and there was clarity. This is how everyone else knew where to go!

I started to plan my homework and do it in advance. I re-read the chapters in the history books we had already studied and read the future chapters we were yet to do.

I saw that history was the story of people, just like in Narnia. I could see pictures of them in my textbooks. Then I realised I could make pictures in my head of what I was reading, like a movie. I looked at the diagrams in the maths and science books. I could see that they analysed and explained the text. This made learning so much easier for me. Suddenly I could picture information in my mind.

Now I had two tools for learning: my ability to connect with the teacher and learn almost via osmosis, and my new visualisation tool. This second tool was very empowering because feeling connected with the teacher was out of my control whereas I could visualise information whenever I wanted and it didn't depend on anyone else or my relationship with them.

My marks went up 40% in every area. In less than 6 months, I went from a very average student barely passing to an exceptional learner at the top of all my classes. My teachers were astounded. Some of them found it hard to believe. But by this point in time I had memorised entire textbooks and could recite huge passages, making my learning undeniable.

Needless to say, I did well in my HSC. I went to university and studied, of all things, English literature! I did a double major in English and Drama and gained an honours degree in English Literature. I then decided to do a Diploma of Education in English and Drama and graduated 'with Distinction', was Dux at The University of Sydney and won the P.R. Cole Memorial Prize for excellence.

The more I studied teaching and despite my success, the more I felt there was something strange about the way I learnt and processed information. So I went to an educational psychologist. He did various tests and then sent me to Westmead Hospital for more. The upshot was that I was diagnosed with dyslexia, ADHD and a condition known as 'Vanishing Memory'.

The assessment for Vanishing Memory was basically a short term memory test. The psychologist put four random symbols in a row. I then looked at them, he covered them over and I needed to replicate them in order from the left to the right. The average person can remember six in a row.

What was interesting to me was that if I could remember them as a pattern, put the two end symbols down first and work my way into the middle, I could remember eight symbols and they would be in the correct order. The psychologist had no interest in this innovative way of remembering information and insisted I had to start from the left and go to the right. Doing it his way I could not even remember four in a row.

I basically had no ability to remember information in a sequence but I had superior capacity to remember information in a pattern. They gave me some drugs for my ADHD that made me feel really angry so I stopped taking them. Then they gave me some antidepressants as an experimental treatment of my ADHD. These made me feel totally euphoric and manic so I stopped taking them as well. I felt I had done exceptionally well working with my mind, rather than with drugs, and maybe I would be better off to pursue that understanding instead.

So that's what I did. In the year 2000 I discovered Neuro-Linguistic Programming, or NLP, and a whole new explanation of learning opened up to me that made complete sense of my experiences. I was so excited that I learnt everything I could within the field. I then began teaching this information and spreading it through my DVD products such as *Focus on Kids* and *Kid's Matrix* because I felt the information was so powerful. Learning and communication styles could give children, teachers and parents practical tools to empower recall and understanding.

Basically the theory in NLP was that each person has a preferred sense they took most notice of and this affects the kind of information they observe and how they process that information internally. This preference also affects body language, speech patterns, learning, recall and behaviour.

So some people take most notice of what they see. They communicate by describing the pictures they see in their head. As a result, they tend to speak quickly as a picture says a thousand words. They also tend to sit up straight so they can see everything. They learn most effectively through diagrams and illustrations. NLP calls them Visual learners. In the story, I translate them into the Tribe-that-Sees-and-has-Visions from the Painted Desert.

Some people take most notice of what they feel and do. They communicate by describing their emotions or through their body memory. As a result, they tend to speak slowly, as it takes time to translate emotions and activity into words. They also tend to sit back in a relaxed manner so they can access their gut feelings. They learn most effectively by connecting with their teacher or by doing an activity. NLP calls them Kinesthetic learners, from the Greek 'kinos' which means 'to move'. In the story, I call them the Tribe-that-Moves-and-is-Touched from the Forest of Rain.

Other people take most notice of what they hear. They communicate by describing auditory information, sounds or through discussion. As a result, they tend to speak melodiously, as they take notice of tone, rhythm and words. They also tend to sit with their head on its side so they can listen more intently. They learn most effectively through what they hear and learning can be enhanced by word games, rhythm and music. NLP calls them Auditory learners. In the story, I call them the Tribe-that-Listens-and-Sings from Echo Canyon.

Finally, some people take most notice of data and calculations. They communicate by describing facts and figures. As a result, they tend to speak in a monotonous tone as they express themselves with little emotion. They also tend to sit straight so they can focus on their thoughts without interruption from their bodies. They learn most effectively through logic, conceptualisation and analysis. NLP calls them Audio-Digital learners. Apart from working things out in their own mind, they will usually read or listen to facts and figures to access information. In the story, I call them the Tribe-that-Thinks-and-Calculates from the City of Concrete.

There is more information about each learning style at the back of the book which you can read to gain more detail. Of course the story itself illustrates each style. The chapters alternate between the points of view of different characters who come from different tribes. You will see how the characters use different senses in their language and how this affects the information they notice, their values and world view.

Most people have a dominant and secondary style of learning and this combination creates greater variety. For me the learning styles explained my entire learning development. I was naturally a Kinesthetic learner and it was easier to learn if I connected with a teacher, had an activity like acting or could connect to the emotions of a character through their story.

Then I happened upon Visual learning as a tool, thank goodness, because it opened up a world of understanding and recall through pattern recognition. It also made a massive difference to my ability to control and direct my own learning.

Auditory and Audio-digital learning were my weak points but by learning NLP, I was able to translate that information into either a pattern or a story to enhance my recall. With information I listened to, I would get a picture in my mind or connect to the speaker to understand their intention or passions. This helped me relate to more factual data. It also assisted my appreciation of those people with a learning preference different from my own because they enjoyed doing tasks I found tedious. This helped me gain valuable assistance from bookkeepers, accountants and financial planners, which has been so important in my business.

In the end, we all have access to all the learning styles. When we under- stand our own and others' preferences we gain tools and ways of seeing the world that would not be available to us otherwise. This in turn creates tolerance and appreciation of difference which makes our experiences so much richer.

No style is right or wrong – they just open up different perceptions which gives us more choices and greater intelligence: intellectually, emotionally and socially. We can adjust ourselves more easily to use the appropriate learning style for the situations we find ourselves in while still enjoying our own unique talents and perceptions.

The best way to use this book is to read the story first, allowing the learning to flow into the subconscious mind and making the skills available automatically. Then read the two sections that follow the end of the story so you can use the skills with more conscious volition. You may also like to share this book with family members, teens and colleagues.

My wish for you is that this knowledge gives you peace of mind about your own way of being in the world and explains many of your childhood experiences. I also hope it allows you to learn more easily while creating greater love and understanding in the way you relate to others.

Thank You

I would like to thank Julia Cameron for her book, *The Artist's Way*. Over 20 years ago I read her book and did the writing ritual she calls Morning Pages, where you write three A4 pages continuously about anything to overcome writer's block. At first my writing was all about how I was feeling at that time which wasn't very good. Then after about three weeks I heard a different voice coming through. The voice said: "I am Wind-in-her-Hair and this is my story." I just wrote down what I heard. Then I allowed life to get in the way and stopped doing Morning Pages. I thought I would write when I had time but of course I never did. In fact it took me seven years just to write the first three chapters!

So it all sat on the backburner until one day my dear friend, Katrena Friel, said she thought it would be great if I wrote a book about the NLP communication styles. I suddenly realised that I could take my story of Wind-in-her-Hair and use it as a parable to demonstrate the communication styles in a creative way. It could then be enjoyed by everyone and bring together the joy I experienced with the Narnia books and these powerful tools for learning. This is how *4 Tribes 1 Earth* was born. Thank you so much Katrena!

I would also like to thank:

Michelle Duval, my extraordinary friend who wrote my foreword and is such an inspiring thought leader. She has taken the communication styles and Meta Programs from NLP to a whole new level of sophistication and application with her Fingerprint for Success programs. I highly recommend them. I love you my dearest friend and treasure all our moments together.

To my designer Kylie Maxwell, you are so incredibly intuitive and it is such a joy to work with you. I love the way you translate my stories into design concepts that are so much more amazing than I could imagine. You allow my spirit to shine through your design.

To Tad James, for teaching me NLP in 2000 and being so supportive of my individuality.

To my avatar designer, Pavel Kosogolov, for bringing my characters to life. To my editor, Meredith O'Rourke, so happy to have you so sensitively edit my work. To my American publisher, Viki Winterton, for taking my books to the world and making it possible to share my passion with a wider audience.

I also want to recognise my father who, even though he died when I was young, told me incredible stories and encouraged me to do the same.

Most importantly, I would like to thank my incredible mother, Elaine McKay, who always encouraged my creativity and made me feel like a genius even though I had issues with traditional learning. I love you so much.

Finally my partner, Will Hickey, who is so loving in his ability to understand and communicate. Thank you for helping me believe again in the power of love.

Pip McKay

SECTION 1

4 Tribes 1 Earth

A PARABLE OF COMMUNICATION AND LOVE

TRIBES AT A GLANCE

Once you identify someone's tribe, then match their behaviour and language to build rapport and understanding.

TRIBE-THAT-SEES-AND-HAS-VISIONS

Body Language
Sit upright
Breath top of chest
Speak quickly
Eyes up
Head upright

Common Words:
See, look, imagine

Possible catch phrases:
Do you see what I mean?
Look here.

TRIBE-THAT-THINKS-AND-CALCULATES

Body Language
Sit middle or upright
Breath middle/upper chest
Speak in a monotone
Eyes down
Head straight

Common Words:
Think, idea, concept

Possible catch phrases:
I don't think so.
That's an interesting idea!

TRIBE-THAT-MOVES-AND-IS-TOUCHED

Body Language
Sit back and relaxed
Breath in stomach
Speak slowly
Eyes down
Head relaxed

Common Words:
Feel, do, grasp

Possible catch phrases:
I don't feel like it
Let's do something!.

TRIBE-THAT-LISTENS-AND-SINGS

Body Language
Sit in middle
Breath middle chest
Speak melodiously
Eyes to side
Head on the side

Common Words:
Hear, listen, sounds

Possible catch phrases:
Sounds good
You're not listening!

👁 Tribe-that-Sees-and-has-Visions
Painted Desert

💧 Tribe-that-Thinks-and-Calculates
City of Concrete

Tribe-that-Moves-and-is-Touched
Forest of Rain

Tribe-that-Listens-and-sings
Echo Canyon

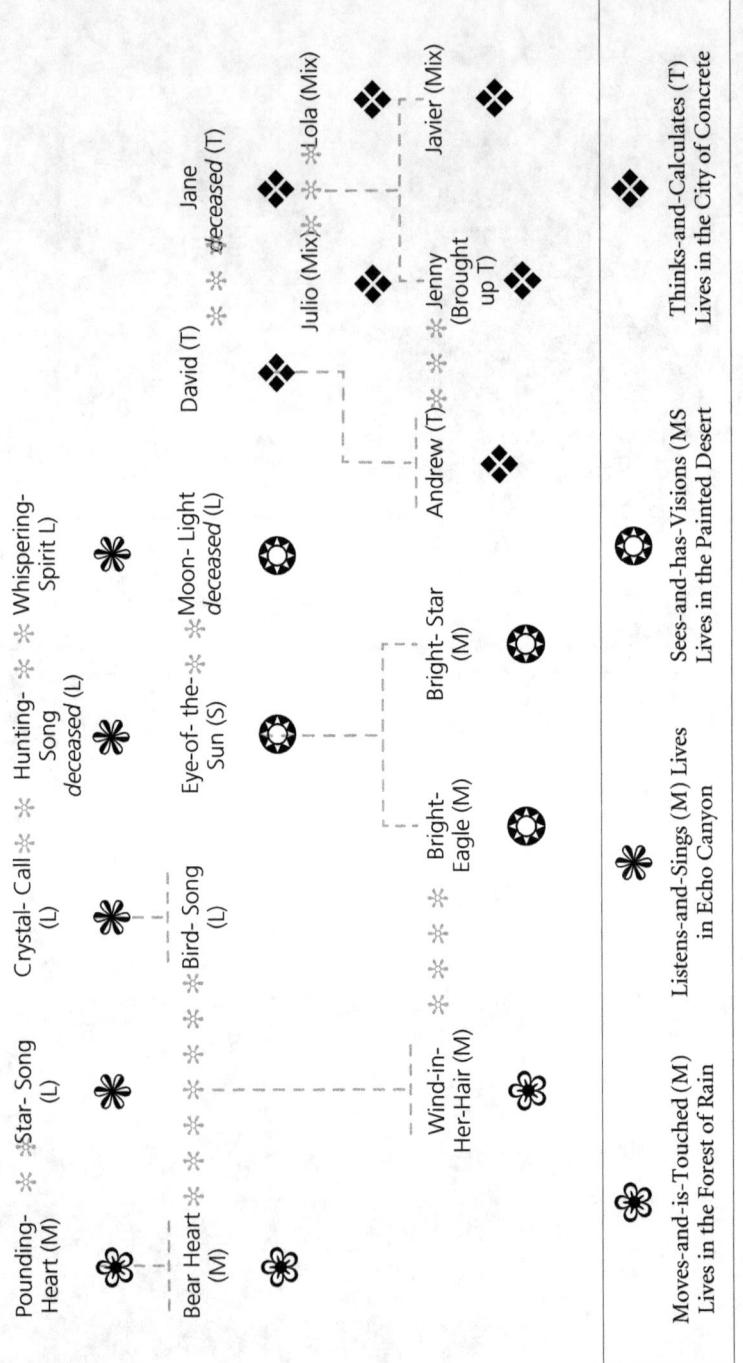

ACT 1

THE STORY OF WIND-IN-HER-HAIR AND BRIGHT EAGLE

Narrated by the Characters

ACT 1, SCENE 1

WIND-IN-HER-HAIR FROM THE TRIBE-THAT-MOVES-AND- IS-TOUCHED

"I won't go and you can't make me," I shouted. I probably shouldn't have, especially since Father had come to me in his position as chief, but he made me so furious. I was a grown woman and could make my own decisions.

"No-one is going to make you marry someone you don't love, my darling daughter," my father said, understanding my heart. "That was not what we said. All we want is for you to consider going to the Tribe-that-Sees-and-has-Visions," he soothed.

"Oh Father, don't try that on me. I know you too well. You would like nothing more than for me to marry Bright-Eagle. Well, I will not go," I said before storming off.

I'd never really had any feeling about marriage before. I had friends who dreamed of nothing else. I had other friends who didn't want to feel trapped. But me . . . nothing one way or the other. That was until now. There was one thing I was absolutely certain about: no one was going to make me marry someone I didn't love.

That was three weeks ago and yet despite my protests, here I was in the desert miles from my own land. I was never quite sure how my father did that. He had a way of making his decisions feel like my own.

I suppose it was because he never really argued and then you had nothing to push against. It felt like he was giving way but actually he was as stubborn as a rock. Yes that's it. A rock in a stream hidden by the water flowing over it. There seems to be movement on the surface but the rock remains exactly in its original position.

Maybe that was why I felt so angry when he suggested that I come here because I knew at some point I'd give in. It's always the same. In the end it just feels uncaring not to. Is that a good thing or a bad thing?

I don't know. One thing I did know: whether I married Bright-Eagle or not, it was now imperative that the tribes began to work together. That meant I really had to make a good impression and do my best to understand this Tribe-that-Sees-and-has-Visions.

So here I am in the desert where the sun is brutal and the dryness has already parched my lips. And walking beside me is . . .

"Come on, there is so much to see." Bright-Eagle interrupted my feelings.

He almost never stopped talking. I didn't have a moment's peace and it was very destabilising. At least Father knew how to give me space so I could get in touch with my feelings.

"Bright-Eagle, I was wondering if, in your tribe, people are ever together without talking?" I asked, hoping he would take the hint.

"What's the point of being together if you don't share your visions? The problem is that words are so limited whereas pictures say so much. So we have to use a lot of words to paint just one picture in another's mind. And I see a lot of pictures."

He certainly does! I suppose I could relate to what he was saying though, about words being limited. I was having my own struggle with language. I had studied his language most of my life. All the tribes in this region believed that it was important to speak each other's tongue. But it seemed impossible to put into his short, sharp words the whirling emotions I felt inside, not to mention the array of feelings I could sense in others. How could all this feeling be expressed in words? Any tribe's words? Why use words at all? Just the touch of a hand was enough to communicate all that was important.

Bright-Eagle's attention had wandered. He was now caught up in the colours of the sunset spreading across the sky. "We will burn in the eye of tomorrow's sun," he observed. "We will need to make an early start." Then he left me without even a glance goodbye.

I felt the familiar tear of departure I always experienced whenever someone left abruptly without touching my arm or warming me with a smile. This tribe was certainly different from my own.

I missed my tribe.

I missed the Forest of Rain. I missed Father.

I even missed sleeping in.

I could feel fat tears forming in my eyes like tree sap. It was so frustrating. I didn't want to feel vulnerable, not here, not where people couldn't understand me.

Maybe Bright-Eagle was right: maybe I was too sensitive.

ACT 1, SCENE 2

BRIGHT-EAGLE – THE GIRL WHO FEELS TOO MUCH

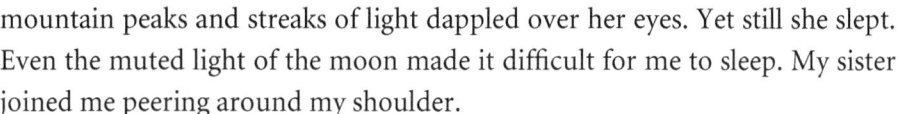

"She can't still be asleep," I thought. I had been looking for her all over the camp but couldn't find her. Everyone else was awake and had already made their morning prayers to the Eye-of-the-Sun. It was my sister, Bright-Star, who suggested that she might still be sleeping. I couldn't believe it but it was the only place left to look. I lifted her tent flap just in case and saw her lying with her arms flung out in surrender and her closed eyes busy in dream visions. The sun had just risen above the mountain peaks and streaks of light dappled over her eyes. Yet still she slept. Even the muted light of the moon made it difficult for me to sleep. My sister joined me peering around my shoulder.

"See, I told you," she said.

"Wind-in-Her-Hair," I called, but still she didn't stir.

"She looks beautiful, if you like that kind of thing, but she's very untidy," Bright-Star observed with a hint of disapproving amusement, which was the total opposite of Bright-Star. Even as a child she looked as perfect sleeping as she did awake.

"I think you're going to have to touch her." Her eyes sparkled with mischief.

"I couldn't, Bright-Star. What are you picturing?" I looked at her, shocked.

"Well, she does come from the Tribe-that-Moves-and-is-Touched. How else are you going to wake her?" She paused, but when it was obvious from the look on my face that I would do no such thing, she said: "Okay I will then."

Her hand shot out quick as lightning and touched her foot. Wind-in-Her-Hair was instantly awake. Bright-Star was right, these are strange people from the Tribe-that-Moves-and-is-Touched. So totally different from us. Touch is not something we would normally do, particularly with strangers.

"Come, we want to show you the Vision Caves before the sun is too hot," I said abruptly and let the tent flap drop.

"I'll be with you, as soon as I can," I heard her murmur sleepily as we walked away.

It wasn't long before we left the shade of the camp and entered the Painted Desert. I was proud to show Wind-in-Her-Hair all the subtle beauty of the different sands. "If you observe carefully you can see that the desert is coloured like a painting and densely dotted with life."

Wind-in-Her-Hair seemed to be completely in a world of her own. She walked slowly and was the last of the tribe. I didn't want us to look lazy in front of the elders, so I tried to hurry her up but she kept lagging behind. Bright-Star would turn, catch my eye and roll her own. It was really annoying.

At one point I turned around to see where Wind-in-Her-Hair was when suddenly I noticed a snake crossing her path. It stopped and its body began to tense up as if ready to strike. I was about to call out to her but without seeing it she stopped, closed her eyes and smiled. The snake relaxed, moved its head away and continued to pass harmlessly by. I shook my head. What was I going to do with this girl?

We climbed the jagged cliffs and finally reached the Vision Caves. I was eager to show her all the variations in pigment that could be created by the different rocks, clays and plants used in the paintings.

"The atmosphere is very still and solemn," she commented. "And yet the pictures feel so alive."

Even though the caves impressed her, it was as if she didn't see the point. Instead of being pleased by her obvious enthusiasm, I was frustrated by her lack of focus.

My father, seeing my unguarded emotions, came closer to me and whispered in my ear, "Make an effort to see things from her point of view, my son. She comes from a tribe very different from our own. Describe the hidden vision captured in the paintings so she can see our culture and customs more clearly."

Sometimes I wished my father wasn't quite so observant. All my life I felt myself to be under his piercing scrutiny. Perhaps that's why they called him Eye-of-the-Sun like the name for our primary God, the Sun. Or perhaps his name created that quality in him.

My mother's observations had been very tender. She always saw something to praise or looked for qualities to encourage, whereas my father's comments always showed up some fault, even though he never directly criticised me. When my mother was alive there seemed to be a balance between my talents and my faults. Now I saw only my glaring flaws. It never seemed to bother Bright-Star. She seemed to ignore it and do exactly as she pleased. She was never affected. I sometimes wondered about that. Was she really not affected or did it just look that way? Or was I more sensitive? How embarrassing – Eye-of-the-Sun's only son and I couldn't keep a straight face. Bright-Star used to say she could read my face like a cave painting.

With a deliberate act of will, I directed my sight towards the paintings again before my insights caused me to feel emotions I wished to avoid, particularly here with the eyes of the whole tribe upon us.

I began to describe the Great Vision of the Tribe and the ancient journey that led us to this land. A land so dry that no one else would want it; a land whose barrenness would keep us safe from the Eye of Envy. Well that was the idea, although it didn't seem to be working out that way now. We'd been a travelling horse-tribe but with just one underground spring to sustain the whole village, we had to let the horses go and wander the land on their own. Then instead of our horse-companion's eyes to help us, we had to rely only on our own. I showed her the picture of the ancient chief, his face hollow with unshed tears, as he shooed away his mythic horse, Rainbow-Rider.

I looked over at Wind-in-Her-Hair. Her face was shining with her own tears but her eyes were unfocused, as if she were looking within. She looked so different from the rest of the tribe whose high cheekbones were dry and stony. It suddenly occurred to me that she really was very beautiful with her huge liquid eyes and dewy skin. She seemed to be making a massive effort to see the world from our point of view. Perhaps Father was right, as usual; it mustn't be easy for her and I probably was too judgemental of her differences.

ACT 1, SCENE 3

WIND-IN-HER-HAIR – THE CAVE OF FEELING

As I stood in the presence of the paintings, I could feel their story reach out and touch me. I could feel the epic journey of tired, heavy bodies that longed for rest and nurture. I could sense the pain, the resigned heart that no longer trusted the intentions of other tribes and searched for a place of peace and safety. I could feel the ripping loss and loneliness as they shooed away their horse-companions to wander the land alone. I began to understand. With all their hardship it was no wonder that they shut out their feelings and focused instead on their future visions. I wondered what it would soon be like for my own tribe. With water becoming scarcer in the forest, we had already sent our bear-friends higher up the mountains to find a flowing stream. It was a time that ripped my father apart but the forest was becoming less and less able to sustain life.

I sensed Eye-of-the-Sun observing me closely. I turned and caught his eye and he nodded almost imperceptibly. Then he turned back to the paintings and I followed his gaze. Everybody began to fall silent.

Underneath the peace of collective breathing I could just hear a faint whispering, although I knew no one was speaking. I gazed at the paintings in a kind of trance and they began to whisper to me of the Soul's Calling, a calling that went beyond experiences and need, to a deeper meaning, a meaning beyond understanding.

My mother had once told me of the still quiet voice that could be heard in things of great power and beauty but I had never really listened before. I had been brought up in my father's tribe, the Tribe-that-Moves-and-is-Touched.

My mother came from the Tribe-that-Listens-and-Sings. I could speak her language and sing her songs but I never really heard in the way my mother described.

She would smile when I told her that and say, "You are your father's daughter," but I knew she didn't mind. She did so love my father.

Well I suppose if my parents could make their differences work, I could at least put in a bit more effort with Bright-Eagle. Who knows what might happen?

I walked back to Bright-Eagle's camp in a different way. Instead of focusing on my own internal emotions and the dancing vibration of the earth, I allowed myself to be touched through my eyes. The vast array of colour from the lowering sun bathed the land in every hue and I found my body strangely vibrant. I was filled with energy but energy gained by focusing outside myself.

I started to notice the way Bright-Eagle looked. His sun-bronzed skin was stretched smooth over his lean, long muscles and the sway of his long straight hair caressed his back. It had never struck me before, his intense physical beauty. Normally I was overwhelmed by how it felt to be beside him. His dancing impatience was very distracting and the lack of internal centre made me feel completely off-balance.

Then for one moment, as I watched him striding slightly in front of me, I realised that I had no contact with my internal feelings. Suddenly I felt a gaping void inside, created by my attention outside myself. Then my feelings rushed in at full force. I became aware of a strange feeling I had trouble recognising. I closed my eyes to get in touch with it. It felt like a loss of connection, an emptiness which disappeared when I opened my eyes and saw Bright-Eagle in front of me. It frightened me.

I reached out and touched his hand.

ACT 1, SCENE 4

BRIGHT-EAGLE – THE GIRL WHO TOUCHED ME

She touched my hand.

It felt like a lightning bolt travelling up my arm and shooting into my temples, obliterating all sight. I closed my eyes. All I could see was the blood red pulsing of my heart behind my eyelids. I was so surprised.

I turned around and looked straight into her eyes. She looked right into my soul. Her eyes were smiling and I felt a joy burst through my chest.

I had never really felt before. My attention had always been outside myself. I wanted to feel again but the moment was over. She dropped my hand and continued walking. Now I seemed to be following her.

I was pleased we were the last of the group returning to camp. I was not sure how this would look to the others. Our elders had always warned us against feelings. "They cloud your eyes and muddy your vision quest," my father would say.

"Watch your feelings," my mother once said to me. "Do not drop into their depths or you will lose your clarity."

What was I to do? Now I could see only her – and how I wanted to touch her – but she kept her head forward and walked quickly on.

ACT 1, SCENE 5

WIND-IN-HER-HAIR – THE CHASE BEGINS

I could feel his intense yearning to touch me again. It was exhilarating. This must be what my father told me about. "Plunge into your feeling," he said. "Open your heart wider and wider but keep him physically at bay. He must chase you to be worthy."

"Oh but Father, he is worthy. He is! I can feel it." How I longed to hold him and touch him again. My heart felt light and painful at the same time. It reminded me of how I felt when Father was away on a long hunt.

"Keep yourself busy or sing," my mother would say. "Savour these moments alone. They strengthen your soul."

So with that in mind I kept walking, longing to turn around, longing to look deep inside Bright-Eagle's eyes again. For once I didn't want to rebel against Father's wishes. This was way too important and if it wasn't for his suggestion I wouldn't be here at all.

Instead, I used my new vision to occupy my time. The more I looked outside of myself the easier it was to ignore my feelings and follow the directions of my parents. After all they had had a long and happy life, from two different tribes.

ACT 1, SCENE 6

BRIGHT-EAGLE SEES HIS FATHER

By the time we came back to the camp, orange and red rays were streaking across the sky and the Eye-of-the-Sun were beginning to wink closed. I had been finding it hard to look at Wind-in-Her-Hair, but I didn't need to look because this new sense of feeling was palpable. I felt that I could reach out and touch our connection. The problem was that when she moved too far away from me, I felt stretched and uncomfortable in my solar heart. All I wanted was to draw her back to me.

These feelings in my body were so disconcerting that I couldn't concentrate. Normally I only felt my body when I was unwell. Even when doing our daily exercises, I never really felt my body. If my muscles burned, I focused on watching them move or seeing visions of the future and the feeling would soon disappear. This allowed us to exercise beyond most tribes' capacity and made our muscles long and lean. We highly prized this look and even the elders kept their bodies slim and their muscles smooth.

Wind-in-Her-Hair looked completely different. Her long hair had a variety of different colours blended together and it waved softly around her face and down to the small of her back. Her hips and breasts were round and her stomach softly curved. Her lips were full and her eyes liquid. Although she was more covered up than our own womenfolk, she somehow looked more naked, almost indecent in the voluptuousness of her body – it was irresistible. Her skin, so soft and smooth, shone as it wrapped itself around her fullness like some ripe fruit. I could hardly control the urge to touch her.

"You look distracted, Son." My father was helping me dress in full ceremonial clothes for tonight's feast.

"I am sorry, Father, my vision seems clouded," I replied demurely.

"To have clarity you must guard against your feelings, my son. Keep clear in your mind the picture of who you are. You are a chief's son and one day you will focus the vision of the entire tribe. At times of heightened senses, when all others lose their way, you must remain focused. This is what it means to be the Chief, the Eye-of-the Tribe, the Focused-One."

"Yes, Father." How did I tell my father, a man who never seemed to have had a single emotion, what was going on inside me? My eyes were only for her and my focus on the lingering touch of her hand in mine.

"Tonight, it is she who proves her worthiness to us. If she can paint a picture with words of her family's story, then she may be able to become a member of this tribe. Her parents' story will allow us to assess if you can share a vision together, or whether your pledge will fade into the darkness."

"Father, I want her to . . ." My words failed me as I realised that I could not express my feelings to my father. His eyes upon me were cold, although his insight seemed clear enough.

"You want her? Your wants have little to do with this, Son. I know it's not easy for a young man. Your eyes are impatient and you like to fill your mind with the beauty you see, but you have responsibilities to the whole tribe. You must choose a wife who can lead as you do, and yet bring a different dimension to leadership. In this way our tribe's vision remains focused but flexible." He broke off his speech interrupted by something he saw in his mind's eye.

"Your mother was such a one. We painted the future of our tribe together. Where I brought burning light, she brought cooling shade. Where I brought textured depth, she brought smooth reflection. I have only seen half a vision since she passed." My father looked down and the shadows covered his eyes so that it was impossible to see his expression. Then he shook his head briefly and looked up straight into my eyes.

"If Wind-in-Her-Hair is to become your wife, she will need to bring that extra dimension to your sight. I see visions of troubled times ahead and we will need new resources if we are to see our way forward. This is why we wish to share our vision with another tribe, as we have done in times past. But we must know that she brings us a strength that adds further to your clarity. She cannot be a distraction."

"Yes, Father, forgive me. I see clearly now."

"Come, Son. I do not wish to be so dark on what has been such a light day. Let your eyes be bright. I see an inner beauty and growing wisdom in Wind-in-Her-Hair. I am sure she will paint well with her words. The Tribe-that-Moves-and-is-Touched is famous for its storytelling and her father is a great man."

ACT 1, SCENE 7

WIND-IN-HER-HAIR CONNECTS WITH THE STORY OF HER PARENTS

I was led to the fire in the centre of the camp. The meal had been completed and I had been bathed and dressed in this tribe's traditional clothes. They were uncomfortable and heavy with beading, but tonight my comfort didn't matter. I knew that this was my rite of passage and a way of introducing the story of my parents to my new tribe.

I could feel leaves flutter in my stomach as my heart pounded but I was used to the swaying flow of emotions and knew to just go with them. Words come to fill stories like fish swimming under the water break free to catch insects. It happens and is natural.

Finally, the rapid visioning music ceased and it was time for me to stand. I closed my eyes and felt for the words as they swam up to the surface of my mind.

"This is the story of my parents and how they met and married." My voice resonated clear and deep. "In our tribe, my parents tell this story together by taking turns to speak. In this way they express their different experiences and feelings of the events that happened. To honour them, I will tell this story as they do, starting from my father's standpoint and then from my mother's.

For a moment, I was distracted by the flash of Bright-Eagle's eyes upon me, but then I felt the tug of the story draw my attention back to the feelings, and the words gently nuzzled my mind seeking to be said.

ACT 2

THE STORY OF BEAR-HEART AND BIRD-SONG

Narrated by the Characters

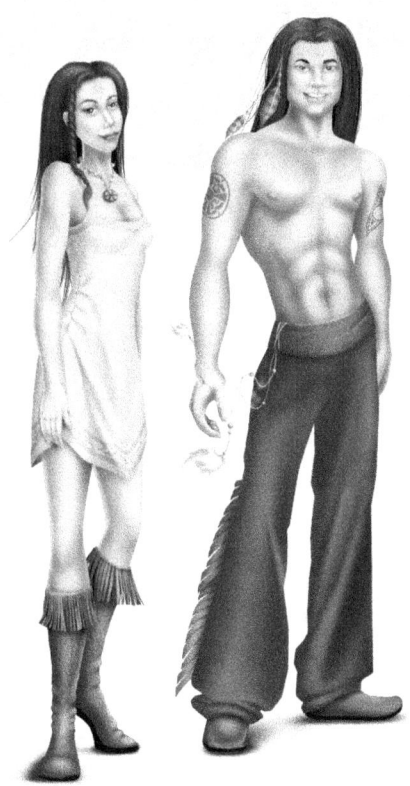

ACT 2, SCENE 1

BEAR-HEART, SPEAKS – HE HEARS THE SONG

Even though I lived in the Forest of Rain with the Tribe-that-Moves-and-is-Touched, I have always wanted to hear the world of sound and the music of the earth. I suppose that's because my mother was from the Tribe-that-Listens-and-Sings. She and my father met at the Gathering-of-the-Tribes that happened once a year in the early days. I don't know why we almost never meet now. I suppose everyone seems to be on a different path these days.

When I was a child, my mother would take my hand and put it to my heart: "Can you feel your heart, my little warrior?" I could feel it beating strong and true. "Now feel it inside your ears, like you hear my voice." But I could not.

"Mother, all I can do is feel my heart under my fingers. How can I feel it in my ears? It's beating under my hand?"

"Ah yes, my darling," she sighed. "You are your father's son. Maybe . . . maybe one day you will hear the music of the body."

Even though I wanted to, I could not hear the music of my body or the earth. My mother could sing like the birds that surrounded us, she could murmur like the streams and sometimes she would sing with such high, haunting beauty that I swear she was talking to the stars, helping their passage through the spheres. I could hear the music of her song and was fascinated by it.

My father's tribe, where we lived, never made music like that. We would drum, chant and dance. You could feel the beat through the earth, matched by the pounding of stamping feet. The vibrating earth made us stamp in time and spin to the rhythm. For my mother though, I sensed it was different. She would sing something she called a melody. When I listened, there was a combining of sounds that was like an ever-changing stream in my ears but when I went to copy the sound, I felt clumsy and the sound clunked out of my mouth. Her sound was like the flutter of eyelashes inside my ears, stirring the deepest, finest part of my soul. It was beyond understanding.

"Mother, where does your music come from? I can feel the difference but I cannot reproduce it. It is beyond my touch."

"Dear Little-Bear," she would say, "it is beyond touch but it is related. You must feel with your ears then take the feeling inside where it touches your soul. When your soul speaks, the music will come out of your mouth and express your spirit."

"Mother, how... how can I do it?" I stamped my feet in frustration.

"Listen to your heart. One day it will speak to you between the beats and in the stillness between activity, there it will open the gate to your spirit. Be patient and still, my Little-Bear, and it will come."

It was impossible to be still. All I wanted was to move, move, move! I liked nothing better than to run and feel the pounding of my feet upon the ground, or hunt and throw my spear or fire my arrow, or hug my friends as we bonded in friendship or fought for status in our group. Every now and then I would lie still before going to sleep, with my hand on my heart. I would try to feel the sound in my ears but just as I reached and strained to hear, I would fall asleep – the day's exertions too much for me.

One night, when I reached the seventeenth cycle of my birth stars, I had a dream. A bright bird was in front of me in the forest. It seemed to beckon me with the tilt of its head and I followed it into a clearing where a stream rushed over a bank of rocks in a tiny, quick waterfall. The bird beckoned me again and I waded into the pool below the rocks. When I was up to my shoulders in the water, the bird dipped its head and sang into the pond. Waves of sound flowed from the bird's mouth and burst through my heart exploding out of my mouth in what I felt, at last, must be song. The exquisite beauty vibrated in my soul and tears streamed down my face. This was my mother's experience. I felt for the first time that I was my mother's son.

When I woke in the morning, I excitedly listened for the sound of my spirit in the silence between the beatings of my heart. But my heart beat so swiftly I could not hear. The more frustrated I became the less I could hear. I felt a loss so deep and an emptiness so profound I thought I would die and doubled over and groaned with pain. My mother, hearing me, asked, "Bear-Heart what ails you, my son?"

"I found my soul, Mother, and the moment I touched it, it flew from my heart. I fear I will never find it again."

"Ah my darling boy, now you are ready. It is simply the call of love. You must seek the one who sings to your heart. Tell me your dream."

So I told my mother my dream. "I know who you seek. She is my third cousin's child born a year after you. They call her Bird-Song and her spirit sings to you."

ACT 2, SCENE 2

BIRD-SONG SPEAKS – SHE FEELS THE SONG

My dreams were dissonant. In the past they had been filled with harmony; sound and melody would reverberate in my mind pure and sweet. Now the fluidity of sound became fluid in my body, whirling in a way that left me confused. I woke again, remembering the touch of his hands imprinting my body, the beat of his heart pounding in my ears, until I rocked my head in my hands. I felt the urgency of his breath on my face, the incessant feel of his mouth on mine, but this was not what shocked me.

Had I not, many times, stopped short a call from the many young men of the tribe? I knew the sound of one who wanted to creep into a growing woman's heart. So far I had been impervious. I would lift my head and tune into a higher vibration and the young men would know that I was beyond them. Their song failed to bring me to earth and disturb me with the cacophony of their desires.

But this dream boy, Half-Brave, his low vibrations called to me and my body rocked in tune with his desire. It was most disconcerting. Who could I tell to calm me? Who would understand? My mother, Crystal-Call, had always told me that love was a song one sang together; different pitches one high one low, harmonising together. "Bird-Song," my mother would say, "listen for one who sings in tune with the vibrancy of your spirit. That's what it was like for your father and me before he passed. Purity of harmony, not passion, is the key."

I did not want to sing with this Half-Brave of my dreams. I wanted to grab him and feel his touch on my skin. I wanted sound to be strangled in my throat while our hearts pounded together, making our bodies rise to meet each other.

Who could I say that to? Anyone? Certainly not my mother. Where did this sense come from that seemed so base in its rhythm?

"Mother, tell me about the Tribe-that-Moves-and-is-Touched."

"Where did you hear of such a thing?" Her voice was strained with disapproval.

"Grandma-Arrow spoke of such things," I replied, my tone deferring to her authority.

"Oh, Grandma-Arrow", her voice softened with the lilt of amusement. "You know Grandma-Arrow is not your direct kin?"

"No?" I was surprised.

"Grandma-Arrow was gifted to us."

"Why?" I asked, curiosity making me unusually direct.

"Sometimes one with gifts is born into the wrong tribe and when this happens they are given to the tribe that calls to their soul. Grandma-Arrow hears the voice of the spirits but she was born to the Tribe-that-Moves-and-is-Touched. Medicine women of her own tribe would feel the land and use that to direct their prophecies, but not Grandma-Arrow. The spirits whisper and sing in her ears and her voice has melody."

"Doesn't the Tribe-that-Moves-and-is-Touched have melody?" I could hardly believe my ears.

"I do not really know. Grandma-Arrow has told me that they have the rhythm of dance and the base beat of the drums but no tune. Seek her if you must know but, Bird-Song, the key to your happiness lies in knowledge of your own tribe, not outside."

ACT 2, SCENE 3

BIRD-SONG IS HIT BY THE ARROW

Grandma-Arrow was quietly humming in time to the rhythmic scraping of her whittling knife as I approached the clearing.

I sat down beside her and she cocked her ear towards me, turning her blind eyes away. "Bird-Song, is it?"

"Yes, Grandmother." She could always hear exactly who approached.

"Come talk with me, my sweet child."

"Thank you, Grandmother." I sat down on one of the logs placed by the fire but I didn't know how to begin. I had not told anyone about my dreams although they had been happening for months now. I felt so tired from the lack of sleep and the dissonance in my spirit, I just sat there and let the silence stretch out and fill the space.

"So, do your dreams trouble you again?" Grandma-Arrow broke the silence.

"Yes, Grandmother." My voice was startled, although you would think after all these years I would be used to the accuracy of her knowing and the directness of her approach. I suppose the difference was that in the past I had never been ashamed of my secret thoughts, but now my cheeks burned.

"Do not worry, hot one," she said, before absently patting my red cheeks. "He is coming."

"Who?"

"The one who makes your heart pound," she said chuckling. "It must be a shock for one like you, who is tuned so finely, to actually feel your body so acutely."

"What do you mean, Grandmother?" I asked cautiously.

"You know when I was young I always felt misunderstood and out of place. I felt I could not truly come from the Tribe-that-Moves-and-is-Touched. Their voices grated on my ears and they moved with such clumsy noise. I would leave the Forest of Rain, its sound of drums, animals and people overwhelming me. I would go to the desert where sound was subtler and I could tune into the stars. I thought myself so refined, but now I miss the encompassing feel of arms around me, hands that cup my face and stroke my hair, and a heart that pounds to my rhythm. There is something to be said for the Tribe-that-Moves-and-is-Touched." Her voice trailed off in tender reminiscing.

"So it is true you come from the Forest of Rain? You are of the Tribe-that-Moves-and-is-Touched?"

"Yes, but don't play coy with me child. You know of what I speak." Her voice was rueful. "You have been touched, have you not?"

"Certainly not," I responded offended.

"In your dreams, my sweet?" she gently enquired.

"Oh yes, Grandmother," I confessed, my voice cracking with tears. "I don't know what to do. I should be ashamed but all I feel is pounding desire. My mother would be so disappointed in me."

"Oh yes your mother, Crystal-Call." She spoke impatiently. "Don't take what she says too seriously. In the end we are all touched. What is sound after all but vibration on the wind touching the drums of your ears? Do not worry about your mother. I am telling you he comes."

"What do you mean, Grandmother? How can he come? A Dream Boy cannot come here. He is the stuff of the mind, insubstantial. How can I touch such a one except in my dreams?"

"Your dreams are a prophecy. Right now I hear his approach in Echo Canyon."

Could it be true? Will he really come? I wondered. Or is Grandma-Arrow's prophetic hearing beginning to fade like the sight of her eyes?

She patted my hand comfortingly. "Do not worry. He comes," she reassured me again, as if hearing my doubt. "His name is Bear-Heart. His mother came from this tribe and, if I remember correctly, he is your 4th cousin. A respectable distance and yet not a complete stranger."

ACT 2, SCENE 4

BEAR-HEART'S HEART ECHOES

For three days I walked through the desert with the heat searing my skin and the cold of the night chilling my bones, even under my bearskin blanket. Finally, I saw the wide, solid sandstone walls of Echo Canyon which were so famed in my mother's stories.

I heard the tumbling water rushing over the rocks in the stream that ran through the centre of the canyon. My water bottle was almost empty and the water inside was hot and greasy. So even though I was exhausted, I ran to the river and waded into its depths. I felt the water swirling around me in relieving eddies of pure bliss.
I gently drew water into my mouth, feeling the ecstatic coolness run down the back of my throat and refresh me from within, taking care not to drink too much too quickly. Then I treaded water in the deep pool created by one of the miniature waterfalls.

All at once déjà vu flooded me with its familiar feeling. Was this not the pool of my dreams, where Bird-Song's spirit totem sang to my soul? So it really was a prophecy, for here was the very pool of my dream. If the pool was real, then maybe Bird-Song was also more than a dream. I swam around exploring the pool with happiness bursting through my chest. When I was satisfied that I had committed every part to memory, I floated on my back relaxing and drinking in the atmosphere, allowing my mind to drift.

What was I going to say when I arrived at the village? I must take care not to offend anyone. My mother warned me that courtship was very strict in the Tribe-that-Listens-and-Sings and much talking was required before the necessary arrangements were made. There was to be strictly no touching of any kind until the marriage vows were complete.

I smiled, amused at the difference between this and my own tribe's customs where everyone said not to touch a lover before marriage but no-one obeyed. After all, it was virtually impossible to communicate the emotions that welled up in one's gut through the cold clarity of words. Then there was also no clear boundary in our customs. Since we sat so close together, family and friends always touched knees and holding hands was common with everyone. Even my male friends could hardly be in each other's presence without a casual arm thrown across each other's shoulders. So if you liked a girl, touching her hand was seen as part of normal manners. Then there is not much difference in touching a knee compared to a thigh, which after all is not much higher. Kissing lips is not much lower than touching noses.

Not in this tribe, my mother had warned. Physical touch was reserved for those you were closest to and only then in moments of absolutely private intimacy. All emotions were controlled and spoken about, analysed and dissected, until one hardly knew a feeling from a thought.

When my mother's marriage had been arranged, my father brought her to meet her betrothed at the Forest of Rain. At that time intertribal marriage was even more rare than in my time. When they met, my father stepped forward and kissed her softly on the lips before drawing her into an embrace before the whole tribe.

Mortified, she had turned to her father whose face was red with anger and humiliation. He began to berate my father. All night they sat and talked. The tribe tried to encourage her father to dance out his emotions but he had doggedly insisted on discussion. By dawn he had understood most of our customs and realised that in our tribe it was the highest form of respect to embrace the betrothed before the tribe and so recognise honourable future intentions. With her father placated, everyone relaxed and the courtship could begin again.

So no matter how difficult it was, I must not touch my love. In a way I was glad. I wanted our moments together to be different from the dalliances I had had in my own tribe. I wanted our encounters to be something more, to work on a vibration higher than just the physical. I wanted to hear the call in my spirit, as I had in my dream.

ACT 2, SCENE 5

BIRD-SONG HEARS THE POUNDING CALL

If Grandma-Arrow was right, my Dream Boy was in Echo Canyon right now. I couldn't wait. So after going with Grandma-Arrow to my mother's house where she would announce my dream, I left. I knew a dream of such importance would take hours of discussion, not just with my mother, but also with Whispering-Spirit, who was the Chief of our Tribe. That would give me plenty of time to go to Echo Canyon without anyone missing me.

As I walked, I wondered what our land would sound like to one who had not heard it before. Near the village, the river that ran through Echo Canyon crashed down a large waterfall and then spread out into a shallow lake fringed with swishing trees. Beyond that there was a ring of echoing cliffs that were a haven for birds and wildlife. I walked along the path and listened to these sounds as if I had not heard them before.

The whisper of the long grass along the path was interspersed with the many different bird calls. Some reminded me of water dripping into a pond, others had a rhythmic melody and still others sounded like people laughing. The run off from the surrounding rocks created water that was full of nutrients. The fish teemed in the lake, jumping and splashing and catching the humming insects with a snap of their open mouths. The frogs were in their mid-mating season and were croaking in competition to find the best mate.

I began to sing the Song-of-the-Lake that brought all these noises into harmony with each other. If you pitched different sounds in a rolling rhythm, then nature's cacophony would begin to harmonise and create the foundation of the song. It was then as if nature settled into a gentle tempo that soothed your soul and heightened your spirit.

Right at the purest point, my song was interrupted by memories of last night's dream; the sweat of his body bathing mine while my mouth reached up seeking to be silenced, his heart pounding in my ears.

My voice cracked.

Into the gap, nature's sounds invaded my ears – naked, wild and raw. I felt overwhelmed. Panic reached into my guts and ripped me apart. I could hardly breathe and my loose dress felt tight. I found myself ripping at the strangling necklace around my throat, seeking release. Heat flooded over me. I bent over suddenly feeling sick, coughing and gasping for air. I sat down abruptly and prayed for help from the Goddess of Sound. "Collect my call, hear my heart, soothe my soul." I chanted over and over again until calm began to quiet my heart's rhythm.

"What am I doing?" I whispered in despair. "Who was this Bird-Song? I do not recognise myself." I began to cry a breathless sound that caught in throaty hiccups. "What would my mother think of me? How could I be so base?" I thought.

But even in the depths of my self-berating, I could feel the call of my Dream Boy like a magnetic pull in my solar plexus and despite my tearing shame, I stood up and kept walking towards Echo Canyon.

I decided to take the high path. That way I wouldn't risk meeting him and I could get a sense of him from a distance. The sun had been high for some time, when I eventually reached the place where the Canyon opened to the desert. The air vibrated in lazy waves of heat like a slow pulse of resonant sound, but my heart was skipping a tripping beat in my ears that made my senses light and alive.

Then I heard him. The sound of his voice drifting and echoing out of the canyon like tendrils of smoke buffeted on the wind. He was singing the Song-of-Approach that was the respectful way of entering our village. His voice was strained with the attempt. I couldn't help smiling. He was doggedly repeating the tune and the words, adjusting them as best he could to make them right.

His voice was a low baritone. It was vibrant like the purring of the big cats that some of the elder cat-whisperers had tamed from the hills, however it was quite tuneless. How sweet of him. His mother must have taught him that song before he came. I was touched, and touched as I was by his song, I wanted to touch him physically.

Slowly and quietly I made my way down the secret path that led to the river. I watched him from behind the reeds. Then otter-like, I slipped into the pool. He was now humming the song to himself. His back was to me. His hair, slick and black, draped like a second skin down his smooth brown back. Normally this song from another would cause me to want to harmonise a response, but I felt no such need. Only touching him would satisfy my yearning.

I slipped naked, silent and invisible into the water. I held my breath and dipped my head. Strangely, under water, I found the song reverberating in my mind. I began to hum the response until our waves of sound collided and seemed to create patterns of light and shade, like the dappled sunlight on the clear sandy bottom of the stream. I swam steadily to where his floating body was suspended vertically in the crystal water. Bubbles clung to his skin and fish caressed his torso in a rainbow of indifferent affection. My touch would be different, completely aware. I reached out my hand and softly caressed the bubbles from his skin.

ACT 2, SCENE 6

BEAR-HEART SILENCES THE THUNDER

It was like a bolt of lightning had seared through the water and pierced my skin. I turned around just as her face broke through the crystal surface of the water shattering light. Her eyes, big and dark, stared at me through fern-like lashes and entered deep into my inner void, but fear fluttered out obstructing her approach. Suddenly I felt inexplicably annoyed, while at the same time my body was responding to her close physical presence.

"What are you doing? Don't touch me," I said, shutting her off and moving backwards away from her while my body silently cursed me.

"What am I doing?" she echoed, shocked. "Are you not Bear-Heart or do you run like Chicken-Legs?"

Her tone, although sarcastic, was melodious and exquisite, her voice lilting like my mother's.

"Bird-Song?" I asked, suddenly curious. "Why are you touching me? I thought …"

"Don't worry, I never will again, Wet-Fish," she said as a flush of colour rose up her throat and tinged her cheekbones pink despite the chill of the water. She turned her back and swam smoothly and silently to the bank and rose out of the water. Drops of water flowed down her back, paused and then gathered momentum down the curve of her small, round behind. My body, well and truly in control of my mind now, swam vigorously towards her.

"Bird-Song, please," I called, but she had already slipped into her dress and strode off. The water seeped through the material in patterns of dark and light as her muscles moved under her dress. Without even a backward glance, she disappeared around the curve of the canyon.

"How could I be so stupid?" I thought, berating myself. I just couldn't match all the expectations I had of this Tribe-that-Listens-and-Sings with the electricity of her touch. I have probably ruined everything.

ACT 2, SCENE 7

BIRD-SONG SQUASHES THE CALL

"How could I be so stupid?" I cursed myself. "I threw myself at him and now what will he think of me? Me of all people, known for my cool aloofness, how could I have fallen for this Dream Boy? Such an illusion. I have created him inside my own head with my own self-talk. He is not real!"

"Why did I even speak to Grandma-Arrow? I should have kept my mouth shut. What would she know anyway? She is just an old woman, not even from my own tribe. Who is she to tell me my Dream Boy is real? If I hadn't gone to her, I wouldn't have gone to the Canyon. Then he would have arrived without my awareness and things could have proceeded with natural decorum. Oh Gods, I can't believe it. It's so humiliating."

"Well no more. If he doesn't want to be touched, so be it. I will not touch him through hands, through eyes, through ears. I will be insensitive, blind and deaf to his presence. That is if I ever speak to him again. Maybe now he won't even come."

The thought of him not coming brought cool tears to dampen my hot anger. I pushed them aside and strode back to the village. All sound was silenced by my humiliation and anger.

"Where have you been, Bird-Song?" My mother found me lying on my bed staring out into space.

"I went for a walk," I said, my voice strained and indifferent.

My mother, usually sensitive to such a tone, was oblivious in her excitement. "We have great news, Bird-Song, Grandma-Arrow deciphered your dreams and believes them to be a prophecy, but perhaps you already know."

"Tell me, Mother," I said, avoiding her question.

"Your betrothed approaches. His name is Bear-Heart, he is from the Forest of Rain and he will ask for your hand in marriage. What do you say?"

"Whatever the tribe declares, my parents announce and the spirits sing, I can but harmonise with their wishes." I recited the formal acceptance, taught to us since we were children, but inside I felt hollow. This was meant to be the happiest day of my life, particularly when he was my Dream Boy but I felt deaf to the song of the heart and mute to the expression of love.

"We must prepare for his approach." Unusual for her, my Mother reached out her hand to me.

"Yes, Mother," I said demurely, taking her hand and following her through the opening. I knew the rituals intimately. Both my older sisters had been married in the last two years. First, a cleansing in the cold waters of Crystal River, hair and body washed, while reed flutes were played close to the water's surface making it vibrate. Then, perfumed oil would be burnt and the scent fanned onto me to the sound of sacred chanting. Once dressed, we would spend time in the Meeting House harmonising our voices until Bear-Heart was allowed to enter our village singing the Song-of-Approach.

"We have sent out the forward party to prepare him and ensure we have the appropriate time we need. Come, sweet, this is a most auspicious day. It will further relations between our two tribes, but you must always remember to act appropriately so that you do not bring shame to our family and culture. It will be up to you to instruct him on our ways, not be tainted by his own. Are you up to the task, Bird-Song?"

"Yes, Mother," I said. It was the first time I had ever lied to my mother. "But Mother, I thought you disliked the Tribe-that-Moves-and-is-Touched?

"My child, one cannot disobey when the spirits have spoken. I will miss our discussions when you leave, but child this is an opportunity to instruct another tribe in our ways. Not many are chosen for this task because it takes a special strength of mind, but you, you have been singled out. The spirits bless us in this, be proud, sweetling. You have been seen as pure of spirit and strong in resolve. A mother could not hope for so much."

"Yes, Mother," I said, resigned. Now I had lied twice.

ACT 2, SCENE 8

BEAR-HEART SINGS THE APPROACH

Two young braves from the Tribe of Echo Canyon accompanied me into the village. I was very grateful since their strong, melodious voices covered the cracking nervousness of my own.

The air was filled with vibration as the rest of the tribe echoed the call of welcome and the very sound of nature seemed to harmonise with the song. I felt moved as the vibration reached my heart and resonated in my chest. Joy washed over me so blissfully that my soul felt at peace and all nerves stilled.

I was bathed in the sweetness of sound. I had found myself.
I had found my song. Suddenly my voice clicked into harmony with the others and I knew unity in a way that is impossible in touch where there are always the boundaries of skin separating one from another. In the song each note twined, joined and fitted together boundless and free.

Tears rolled down my face as the chief of the tribe, equally moved, came towards me. He bent his head and whispered: "You are welcome, Bear-Heart. I am Whispering-Spirit, chief of this Tribe. This is Bird-Song's Mother, Crystal-Call. Bird-Song's Father has passed. If you have any questions then address us, not Bird-Song directly. This way you will ensure that your quest is blessed." He smiled at me and I looked around the sea of faces, wet with tears and blissfully at peace.

Then I saw her face, dry and stony like the desert, her eyes cast down and her jaw clenched. All joy left me and my voice cracked as I bent down and whispered back to the chief: "Thank you, Whispering-Spirit, Father of this Tribe. I am truly blessed."

Catching the oddness of my tone he looked up at me and then at Bird-Song. Then he made a small guttural sound of disapproval in the back of his throat and led me into the village. I followed, feeling Bird-Song's stony presence behind me like a weight in my heart.

ACT 2, SCENE 9

BIRD-SONG CALLS TO HER FATHER'S SPIRIT

"Bird-Song, is there something that you wish to tell me?" Whispering-Spirit had caught me unawares, just outside the Meeting-House. The rest of the tribe had settled into a meditative chanting song. Since people were still coming back and forth preparing for the feast, it had been possible for me to make excuses and get some fresh air outside.

I felt exhausted. Anger and separation from the tribe's harmony was taking its toll on me. The brittle pride created a shell of jagged protection around my soul and I felt detached.

"No, Whispering-Spirit. Nothing of which I wish to speak," I said quietly, my eyes lowered.

"So you mean that there is something wrong but you do not wish to speak of it?"

"Yes, Whispering-Spirit. That is right."

"Bird-Song, your father was my best friend. Even before he passed I considered you like a daughter. Can you not find it in your spirit to tell me what is troubling you?" he said. "No matter what the prophecy, I would not have you unhappily married. If you do not wish to marry Bear-Heart, it will strain relations between our tribes, but I would prefer that than to see you so disconnected."

Whispering-Spirit had never spoken with me like this before and his words touched me. I felt my soul flutter, seeking escape from its new cage.

"You honour me, Whispering-Spirit, and your words express great kindness. I am ashamed of my dissonant spirit and do not deserve your concern. Please put such thoughts from your mind. I am happy to do as the tribe declares, my parents announce and the spirits sing," I said, addressing the sadness in his voice.

I had not thought of my father for many years; after the grief had subsided, my mother asked us to put his name aside and not speak of him. She said that the sound of his name was too painful and she wished her mind to be clear so she could hear her thoughts again. We had done so in deference to her wishes. The silence in conversation had silenced my inner thoughts and slowly my emotions had ceased to speak to me as well. But silence does not mean healing.

Suddenly I realised that on this day my father would have played a major role. The ritual recognised that I would move from the shelter of my parents' home and create my own with my new husband. My sisters had asked their fathers-in-law to answer the call required by the ritual, but I had no one. I felt lost like a child again, when the pain and emptiness was heavy in my soul.

I reached out and touched Whispering-Spirit's hand. It was very forward of me and was the first time I had ever touched him. To my relief, he did not pull away but simply squeezed my hand in a reassuring response.

"Please, Father of Our Tribe. It would quiet my spirit greatly if you would answer the call within the marriage ritual," I finally managed to ask.

He let out a small, sad sigh and in a low, liquid voice he answered: "You do me great honour, Bird-Song. It would be my privilege. Your father would be proud of you."

Would he? I thought, but managed to give Whispering-Spirit a trembling smile.

ACT 2, SCENE 10

BEAR-HEART LISTENS TO HIS HEART'S DESIRE

The marriage ceremony was beautiful. It had a sacred energy like everything about this tribe. My own tribe's ceremony was also very special but the dancing and the touching of hands that formed the centrepiece of the ritual, could not unite everyone in the same way.

In this ceremony, the singing created total unification between the individual and the group. There were still distinct parts of calling and answering, like in the Song-of-Approach, but the majority of the ceremony was a trance-like combining of sounds. I found it spiritually blissful. I had never felt spiritual before. Everything had always been physical and I had not been able to bridge the gap between the tangible and the invisible. Now my spirit soared. I could feel it in my body, hovering between the vibration of emotion and thought, sitting in the silence between the beats of my heart, just like my mother had said.

Bird-Song, however, remained indifferent; she sang in whispers during the chorus and only raised her voice when the ceremony required her solo response. We only touched once within the entire ceremony and that was when our hands were bound together with coloured cloth. I don't know what I expected – at least some echo of the electricity I had felt in the pool. Instead her hand was limp, cold and clammy like a dead fish. I wondered if she would ever forgive me.

That night the tribe made a channel of sound leading to our new home. With our hands still bound we walked between the two rows of singing voices. I felt bathed in vibration and blessings. Finally we entered our new home and were alone. The sound of the tribe faded behind us as they slowly dispersed. Bird-Song efficiently untied our hands, took off her outer robes and curled under the woven rugs away from me.

"Bird-Song, I know you are angry with me and truly I behaved abominably but you took me by surprise. I just wanted to honour your ways and show respect." I lent over her, quietly caressing her with my words, though I dared not actually touch her.

She gave no response and in truth her stony back was eloquent enough. Well, it had been a long day. I lay down next to her with my back turned. Two could play at this game I thought as I began to drift off to sleep. Just before falling into unconsciousness I thought I heard quiet tears but I was already too far in the netherworld and I fell into grateful oblivion.

ACT 2, SCENE 11

BIRD-SONG'S HEART CRIES

Really it was silly of me to be so angry with him. In truth I was angry with myself but I just couldn't let go of wanting to blame him. I knew the moment I did, I would dissolve into tears. My pride simply wouldn't allow me to be so vulnerable in front of him again. It would feel like dying. But the moment he turned away I felt the echo of my own hurt reflected back at me and abandonment's black wings smothered my pride.

I remembered that same feeling when Father passed; the dead weight of shock suffocated me into numbness. I remembered how I couldn't cry because to cry meant recognising the truth of our loss. So we sang, my mother, my two sisters and me. We sang until we felt calm and I did feel calm. That was until they brought his body back. He was broken from the fall. His face was disturbingly peaceful while his limbs were bent at incongruent angles. Still I didn't cry but when we pulled his limbs back into place for burial, the cracking sound they made was so lifelike that it made tears rolled down my face, hot and thick like honey.

I couldn't give this Dream Boy those tears. I struggled to hold them back, my breath quietly laboured. I wondered how long it could go on like this, the emptiness inside and the sense of separation. Everything had been so simple before I began dreaming of this Half-Brave. I had been able to control all my feelings and listen to my thoughts, clear and ordered. I could obey my mother, honour my tribe and distain anyone who showed a lack of restraint. Now I was being punished for my pride. Even in the Tribe-that-Listens-and-Sings, sound-meditation and thought-control did not make us gods.

I heard Bear-Heart's breathing lengthen and I knew he had fallen into deep sleep. Slowly I lifted the blanket and slipped silently from our bed and into the restless night. I wondered aimlessly through the sleeping village listening to the night noises. The gentle cooing of new lovers and the murmuring of long-established couples blended with the deeper growls of dreaming dogs and the hunting call of night birds. I wandered out of the main village and found myself drawn to the crackling sound of Grandma-Arrow's cooking fire. Then I heard her singsong voice talking earnestly with someone. But who? I strained to hear. Yes, it was Whispering-Spirit's deeper resonance. They were locked in conversation. I stood stock still, listening.

"Her mother was always a brittle woman, hard to please," said Whispering-Spirit.

"Yes, but she did love Bird-Song's father and there was much private tenderness between them." Grandma-Arrow was one of the few people who could speak her mind, unguarded and without protocol, to Whispering-Spirit.

"Bird-Song's nature is different from her mother's and yet I hear her use her mother's tone. It smothers her spirit's call. She has depth and the capacity to listen beyond her mind's deceptive influence."

"You are too harsh on Crystal-Call. Her suffering makes her brittle. She simply did her duty. A duty set down by your tribe. You cannot make rules and then judge those who obey them, Whispering-Spirit." Her voice rippled with irony making Whispering-Spirit smile at his own hypocrisy. It was one of the things Grandma-Arrow admired about Whispering-Spirit – his ability to see his own weaknesses and be amused.

"Are you always right, Grandmother?" Whispering-Spirit deferred, laughing.

"Only when listening to others. In my own affairs I am quite blind." She smiled, turning her unseeing eyes towards him and looking directly into his soul as if she could indeed see.

"Hmm, I suppose that is why we need others to communicate openly with us, even wise-women and tribal chiefs."

"Yes, it keeps our pride in check, does it not?" she rejoined, "but let's talk of the real cause of your irritation with Crystal-Call."

An involuntary exclamation of shock escaped Whispering-Spirit's lips and the amusement left his voice.

"Of what do you speak? Remember to whom you speak."

"Oh come, what will you do? Have me whipped? Put me over your knee and spank me? Excommunicate me? You never know I may enjoy any or all of those options." Whispering-Spirit could not help but smile at her irreverence. "There is no need to hide from me, Whisper. All hearts' secrets speak to the blind."

"No, I will not speak of it. It is too painful. The wound still screeches open and is raw even after all this time."

"Oh, you are a stubborn tribe. Sometimes I long for the Tribe-that-Moves-and-is-Touched where pride never overshadowed love. It is not principled to martyr yourself and those you love into loneliness."

"This is something of which we will not speak! Is that clear? Crystal-Call followed principle instead of love. Her love for her parents was greater than her love for me; so do not speak of martyrdom to me. I would have sacrificed all." His voice cracked with emotion and he fell into a laboured silence.

"It was a long time ago. She was young. She did what she thought was right, but you, in full maturity, cannot find it in your heart to forgive."

I couldn't believe what I was hearing. Had my mother been in love with Whispering-Spirit? Had she obeyed her parents and married my father, the man her parents had chosen for her, instead of the man she loved?

How awful would it be to marry a man you did not love, especially when you loved another? No wonder my mother was so cold. She had spent a lifetime suppressing her feelings in order to be obedient to her culture's dictates. How different was it for me? I had literally married the man of my dreams and here I was behaving just like my mother. Or perhaps more accurately like a spoilt child. I certainly did not want to martyr myself and Bear-Heart into loneliness.

"Do not push me, Whistling-Arrow. I am Chief of this Tribe and you, you are merely a visitor."

"And you do me great honour by gracing me with your presence." Grandma-Arrow's voice dipped from irony into sarcasm, a transition not lost on Whispering-Spirit. Her eyes met his, again unseeing yet seeing.

"Hmph!" The guttural sound was his only reply.

"So we are agreed then," Grandma-Arrow continued. "Bird-Song should do nothing more than follow the example of her elders and be cold and unforgiving since that is your tradition," her voice was now positively dripping with sarcasm. "Especially since it is one perfected by the chief of the tribe."

Whispering-Spirit had had enough of open communication for one night: "For the moment, goodnight, Whistling-Arrow."

He abruptly rose and I heard his footsteps coming directly towards me, but I was too shocked to move.

Suddenly, a warm arm wrapped itself around my waist and before I could cry out in shock, a hand muffled my mouth and I was drawn away from the path and behind the trees. Whispering-Spirit strode rapidly past without his usual grace and care, deaf to all sound but the raging voice inside his head.

Even before I turned I recognised the touch of my Half-Brave, as it had been in my dreams every night. He removed his hand from my mouth and cupped both around my face. I managed to smile before he kissed me and I felt the softness of his lips rip down the cage around my heart and touch my soul.

ACT 2, SCENE 12

WIND-IN-HER-HAIR COMPLETES THE STORY

"So this was the story of my parents. They stayed in Echo Canyon for two years until my father had mastered my mother's language and customs. Then my mother, wanting a baby, decided that she could be more in touch with her body in the Forest of Rain. So they travelled to my father's tribe bringing a blend of music and dance with them. They were welcomed with open arms although their music was, at first, little understood.

"I was born a year later and although I was greatly influenced by the Tribe-that-Moves-and-is-Touched, I also learnt the art of song and found great peace in harmonising with the forest, the birds and the stars. My mother was happy and content while my father often spoke of Echo Canyon with wistful longing. As chief of our tribe, however, he had too many responsibilities to return. With my mother's influence, the Tribe-that-Moves-and-is-Touched gained much from the Tribe-that-Listens-and-Sings and we were encouraged to speak both languages fluently. We were inspired to discuss ideas, listen and sing as well as communicate our emotions and be physically active.

"So my lineage unifies the best of both tribes and now I bring these resources to combine with those of Bright-Eagle – that is if you deem me worthy and my story well painted. If we are blessed with children, then all three of the great tribes' gifts would be united in one. In these troubled times we can share our gifts, and new potentials and capacities will be born. A fresh bond would be forged between us so that we can unite against the challenges we face.

"This, however, is not the reason I wish to marry Bright-Eagle. My father said I must marry only where my heart calls and I see in Bright-Eagle a Great Spirit that speaks to me – heart, body and soul."

ACT 2, SCENE 13

BRIGHT-EAGLE WANTS HIS BRIDE

I had sat mesmerised by Wind-in-Her-Hair. Her grace, her openness and the beauty of her story made me feel things I had never experienced before. At the last line, the colour rose in her cheeks as she searched for my eyes, looking for reassurance and was, for the first time, vulnerable. I stared right into the depth of her soul and smiled. I was just about to stand up and grab her, not caring what the tribe thought, when all of a sudden my father did a most unusual thing. He stood and clapped. It is not our custom but since he was the chief, everybody did the same.

"Wind-in-Her-Hair, you have woven the picture of your story with great beauty and we honour you with your custom of clapping hands. You are welcome in our tribe. Sit beside me," announced my father.

I was astonished. Even Bright-Star looked at me with her mouth open and her eyebrows raised. Never in our lives had my father given anyone such praise, particularly not us. I should have been pleased that my father was showing Wind-in-Her-Hair such great honour but I just felt annoyed. Yet again he was taking over. Didn't he trust me to show her appropriate appreciation? Sometimes I wished that my father was not the chief of the tribe and then Wind-in-Her-Hair and I could have some private time together. I could hardly wait a moment longer.

There were more stories. They seemed endless. Each seemed duller than the last. The only spark of interest was a story Bright-Star told about a little eagle who tried to leave its nest before it could fly. Trust her to tell a story like that. Well at least it was kind of amusing, not that I felt much like laughing. Wind-in-her-Hair was deep in conversation with my father. The firelight flickered on the curve of her hips under her ceremonial dress and caressed the smooth roundness of her arms as she gestured. She used her hands a great deal when she talked as if her emotions couldn't be contained in her body. Her hands had a particular grace.

Then she threw back her head and laughed. We would actually consider that quite undignified but the unaffected, naturalness of the movement made the air stick in my throat. Then she did something that did make me choke. As her head came back from the laugh, she unconsciously laid her hand on my father's arm.

The whole tribe stopped to watch and held its breath like one living being.

Only the Chief's wife, my mother if she was still alive, was allowed to touch the chief, and even then not in public, but my father seemed at ease. He chuckled and patted her hand, which seemed to linger before their fingertips parted.

The gesture ripped me apart.

What a hypocrite! How could he? For all those years he warned me against feelings and touch, then he does it himself with my prospective wife! It was unbelievable. How many times had he criticised me for unguarded emotions or brushing against someone by mistake? For Gods' sake, he would hardly let my own mother touch me and now this!

I could feel blood rush to my face as a sense of rage bubbled up inside. This would be an enormous insult if it was anyone else in the tribe but to be publicly humiliated by my own father, it was too much.

I stood up and with a raised voice that burned with suppressed rage said: "Eye-of-the-Sun, you humiliate me in front of the entire tribe."

The smile vanished from my father's face. The rattle and chanting stopped. Wind-in-Her-Hair looked at me confused.

"Son, despite how it appears, I do no such thing. Wind-in-Her-Hair has customs very different from our own. As leader of this tribe, it is my duty to make her feel at home, especially in these early stages when she doesn't understand our customs." His voice seemed calm but I watched his face twitch in frustration.

I couldn't hold back and the words that had been bottled up burst forth. "I have watched you, Father. You pretend to arrange my marriage when you really want one of your own."

"Careful what you say, Bright-Eagle. Son or no son, you cannot insult the Chief without repercussions."

"What repercussions, Father? Do you think I shrink from challenging you, when you make a mockery of all you have taught me?"

Wind-in-Her-Hair stood up: "Bright-Eagle, what are you doing? This is foolish jealousy."

"You flirt with my own father and I am meant to simply sit here and take it. My own mother would not dare touch the Chief, her husband, in public and here you are laying your hands on him. But what's worse, he reciprocates. It's one thing for you to make such a mistake, but him . . ."

"Bright-Eagle, please. If I have done something to insult your tribe, I did not mean to. I am still new here. Everything I do I have to measure the response, sometimes when I am tired or excited I simply forget. Please understand. This is what my parents' story taught me, to compensate for our differences. Can we not enjoy the same lesson without the same pain?" Wind-in-Her-Hair pleaded and I could see Eye-of-the-Sun watching me carefully.

The rush of excitement and nerves began to fade as I started to see her point of view. But what of my father? Why was he making allowances for her when he spent the evening telling me that she must prove herself to us, not the other way around?

With his usual insight, Eye-of-the-Sun turned to me: "Things are not always as they look, Bright-Eagle. This is what you must learn to be chief. You must see each experience in its context. Wind-in-Her-Hair proved herself with her story. Now it is our turn to make allowances for her. Such a story has earned our respect."

I knew I should apologise, to push down the burnt pride and the pain in my solar mind, but I simply didn't want to. My mother and I had spent our whole lives making allowances for this man and his position. I simply could not stomach it any longer.

"Your father is right, Bright-Eagle. It's what my parents have always taught me." Wind-in-Her-Hair persisted.

It was more than I could take, her supporting my father.

"Please do not say another word, Wind-in-Her-Hair. You don't know what it was like. You grew up in a family where emotions were prized and all communication was seen as valid. No one in your family cared how things appeared to others. Do you know what it is like to spend your whole life suppressing your emotions because of how it may look? My mother died, dried up through lack of touch. Do you know what it is like not to touch your mother when she is dying? Do you know what it is like for her to be a beautifully decorated living skeleton, dying in silent agony? No, you don't. So don't tell me that my unloving, unaffectionate, unmoved father is right. He believed that it was right not to cry in public when the only person I loved left for another world. Wind-in-Her-Hair, do you understand me, can you feel this?"

I caught her eye for one moment but all I could see was shock. I stumbled away from the circle of the tribe and began to run as fast as I could into the desert, the humiliation and indignation bursting from my eyes in a torrent of tears.

Before Wind-in-Her-Hair had come to my tribe, life had seemed extremely simple. It was much easier to live life untouched by emotion but I didn't want to any more.

ACT 3

THE STORY OF ANDREW AND JAVIER

Narrated by the Characters

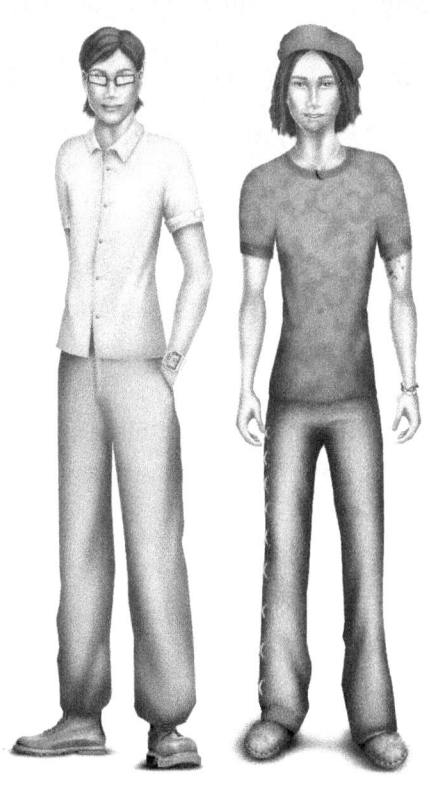

ACT 3, SCENE 1

ANDREW FROM THE TRIBE-THAT-THINKS-AND-CALCULATES

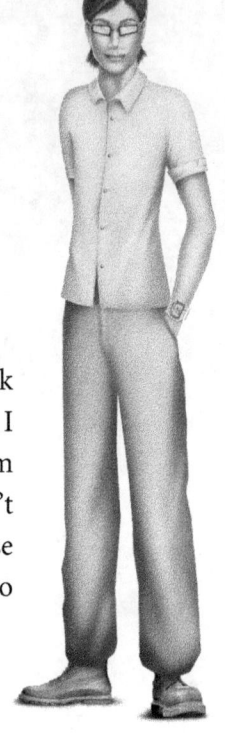

I had always been interested in tribes, ever since I took Anthropology as an extra subject at university. At the time I was amazed at how different tribal culture was, not only from my own, but also from each other. Up until that point I hadn't been interested in the way other people thought. I suppose that was because I had so many of my own thoughts to occupy my time, but after Anthropology I became obsessed. So when my supervisor said there was a chance to study rainfall in what the tribal people call, the Forest of Rain, I decided to volunteer.

I just didn't count on the trip being such a nightmare. First, there was the commercial plane where one engine then another shut down and we had to turn back to the airport. Then, after lengthy delays and a new plane, we finally arrived at a tiny country airport, only to take to the air again this time in what appeared to be a biplane. I didn't know they still existed, I think the last one was built before World War II.

When the jeep arrived to take us to the forest, I thought it must be a joke. It didn't look like it would get us a few miles, let alone all the way to the forest. I knew we would have to go through the desert and didn't fancy getting stuck out there. I should have just refused, but my translator seemed so cool, in a very 'Che Guevara' kind of way, that I didn't want him to think I was some kind of frightened geek.

Well, jeeps might look cool in all those M*A*S*H re-runs but they are definitely not fun to drive in – particularly uncovered through the desert! So now I found myself stuck in the middle of nowhere, with a broken jeep and very little water.

At least I had my translator, I suppose. The sun was going down and the temperature was dropping very rapidly. I would have been cold if I hadn't had the foresight to bring along a decent jacket, scarf and hat – just in case. I have always found 'just in case' an extremely useful concept.

Even though I was attempting positive thinking, it wasn't working. The less water I had left, the more despondent I was becoming. The translator guy wasn't much of a talker, so it was just me and my gloomy thoughts to occupy my time. That was until I heard the rapid beating of drums and rattle. Now this could be interesting.

I had read that the people of the desert were sunworshippers. Perhaps we were coming across the famous Sun Dance festival. I'd always wanted to see one. My lecturer said that very few non-tribal people had ever attended a real Sun Dance festival. There was hippy stuff for tourists in the deserts closer to the cities but not out here. You could only go to one if you were invited and this tribe had almost no contact with modern culture at all.

In fact in this region I only knew of three tribes that lived in the old way, all very different but all connected strongly with the land. They still had no electricity or running water. Apparently these tribes believed that modern culture made the spirit weak and they wanted to have nothing to do with it. Well, I could understand their point; I hadn't seen any evidence of modern culture helping tribal culture in any way at all, and that's an appalling understatement.

Then just as we started to get closer, this guy burst away from the gathering and ran like the speed of light right towards us. My translator motioned me behind a rock, which we ducked behind just as this guy ran straight past us and out into the desert. Then he broke down into tears. My own problems seemed to vanish in the face of this guy's intense suffering. I had been told that the desert people were very proud and unemotional, so there really must have been something terrible going on.

Then the strangest thing happened. This girl appeared out of nowhere running after him. She looked completely different from him and seemed totally out of place in the desert, like she had come from another world. She was really beautiful; well I suppose if I was to be objective, they both were, but so different. She was as round and voluptuous as he was tall and slim. Even though she was much curvier than he was, she was just as swift. She ran like the wind and seemed to defy gravity.

Finally, she reached him, wrapped her arms around him and began singing. Her voice was so exquisitely beautiful that, if I wasn't a scientist, I could have sworn that the night noises paused and then harmonised with the sound. His heaving sobs subsided and he wrapped his arms around her waist and they rocked together. Finally, as he became calm, she stopped singing and they began murmuring together, something I couldn't hear and would not have understood anyway.

I did think that perhaps I was kind of intruding. It was, after all, a very private moment but I was so curious I could hardly tear my attention away. My translator was obviously the better man as he wordlessly pulled me by the arm and led me away.

ACT 3, SCENE 2

JAVIER TRANSLATES

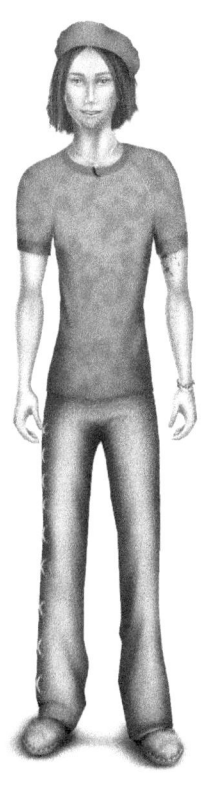

Really it is incredible how insensitive and intrusive some of these scientists are. You would think that after all these years translating for them that I would be used to it by now but it never ceased to amaze me. Then they write about the tribes as if they were being objective. As if the tribes don't tell them what they want to hear. They think they come here to study the tribes but they never do. They come here to feel again. That's why they all want to go to the Forest of Rain, however there's much wisdom to gain from all the tribes. I wish they could learn to look and listen with sensitivity as well, but of course they don't. They look through the lens of their own culture and hear what they want to or the chatter inside their heads.

The Tribe-that-Moves-and-is-Touched was very patient. Bear-Heart once told me that it was their spiritual duty to educate the scientists that came, so long as their presence didn't affect their culture. I suppose, in truth, better a scientist than a tourist.

This time though it had been different. Bear-Heart specifically requested a young scientist to come and study the Forest of Rain and they chose this wide-eyed mooncalf. I don't know what they were thinking. Maybe Bear-Heart thought a younger man would be more open – less ego to overcome. Well, we will have to see, one never knows. Strange things happen to people in the Forest of Rain.

The last anthropologist who went there wrote a bunch of books about his experience and now he's a 'spiritual teacher'. I wonder what Bear-Heart really feels about that. Mind you, he is so gracious he would never say. He doesn't like people to feel uncomfortable or perhaps it's just that he understands people so deeply that he always knows where they are coming from.

I've never met such a man as Bear-Heart. Truly a great leader. Well actually, all the tribal leaders were amazing people; wise and enlightened. I wonder if there will be any more like them in the future. I certainly hope so. Maybe that is why I keep coming back. I hope to absorb as much as I can in case one day it just disappears.

ACT 3, SCENE 3

ANDREW MEETS THE TRIBE

The translator said it wouldn't be a good idea to enter the village right at this moment. When I asked him why, he said that the man who just passed us was Bright-Eagle, the Chief's son, and that there must have been some major event for him to behave like that. So we waited in the freezing desert for about two hours. It was excruciatingly boring. That was until I remembered that I had my phone. There was no reception but at least I could play some games until the battery died. Then there was literally nothing to do.

The translator guy just lay on his back looking at the stars completely content – it was really annoying. He didn't make any effort at conversation. The only thing I found out was that his name was Javier and that he knew all three of the local tribes and their languages. After answering my questions, he went back to staring at the stars without asking me a single question back, which seemed really rude.

"Let's go," Javier said, after what seemed like a lifetime. "Why now?" I asked.

"The feelings have settled," he said.

The feelings have settled? How would he know that? But with absolute certainty Javier walked towards the village. I don't know how he could see in the dark. I kept tripping over things and stubbing my toe. I should have brought my hiking boots but I had reasoned that they were very heavy and I wanted to travel light, which wasn't easy with all the other "just in case' things I had brought.

Finally, we reached the centre of the village where there was a clearing and a fire that was dying down. A strikingly beautiful older man sat cross-legged, staring into the fire. Javier took a thick hand-rolled cigar out of his jacket. The tobacco was roughly wrapped in leaves of some kind. Javier knelt down by the fire, lit it and drew on it until it was smoking on its own. The smoke was fragrant and obviously didn't have tobacco in it as I had first thought. I suppose it was some kind of ceremonial herbal cigar, something like a peace pipe. I started thinking how cool it would be to smoke my first 'peace pipe equivalent' with an authentic tribal leader.

Javier handed the herbal cigar to the older man who, without looking up, took the offering. I didn't really know what to do, so I sat down. Both men ignored me, passed the cigar between each other and entered into a conversation I couldn't understand.

ACT 3, SCENE 4

JAVIER SEES THE SUN

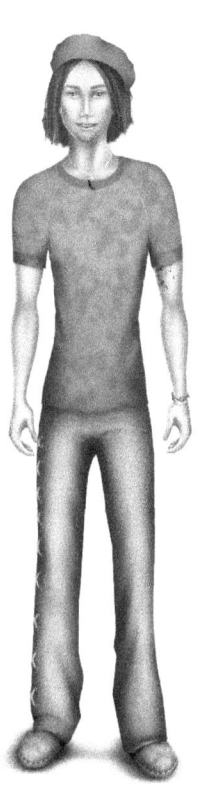

"Please forgive us, Eye-of-the-Sun. We disturb your visioning," I said. This was going to be awkward. I had never brought a visitor to this tribe. Eye-of-the-Sun had made it clear that they would not be welcome.

"As always, we are happy to see you, Javier. But why the foreigner? This is not a good time. The vision of the tribe is fractured," he responded.

"Our jeep broke down in the desert. We were heading to the Forest of Rain but have few supplies."

"Why does Bear-Heart see these people?" Eye-of-the-Sun's voice betrayed his annoyance but his face remained impassive.

"It is different this time. Bear-Heart requested to see this boy scientist."

"Why would he look for such a thing? These foreigners see what will increase their status and profit. There is no true visioning in them."

"Please excuse me. It is not my place to say what vision Bear-Heart has for his tribe. I can only let you know what I see from my own observations." Eye-of-the-Sun nodded and I continued. "There has been little rain, the forest is browning and the life-force of the trees vanishes into the sun. Bear-Heart seeks answers from those he considers responsible."

My language was rusty and awkwardly formal. This tribe had a very distinct way of speaking. They painted pictures with their words and they spoke really quickly. I was out of practice. Recently, I had spent more time with the Tribe-that-Moves-and-is-Touched. They speak much more slowly and one has a sense of almost tasting the round sounds of the words inside your mouth, like eating some juicy fruit.

"He seeks advice from a boy?" Eye-of-the-Sun interrupted my thoughts.

"I think he looks for a language that the world outside the tribes can understand. He feels a great, wrenching sadness for the forest. Old trees wither and die and the glacial ice on the mountains that feed the streams is shrinking," I explained. There were not many words for feelings in this language. Those they had were used only for special occasions of grief and had great power.

"The light of life in the forest fades. We see it here too. We are used to dryness but over the last years even the little rain we expected has disappeared. We are fortunate that the underground river still feeds our oasis." His voice was resigned. "Very well. You can eat and then rest here tonight. Tomorrow we will find you a guide to show you the fastest way to the Forest of Rain."

We were fed and shown a place to sleep. Eye-of-the-Sun didn't move but seemed to be keeping vigil by the ceremonial fire. I couldn't sleep; the air was restless with unspoken emotion. Just before dawn, I felt a need to get up and walk around.

Suddenly, from the desert, I watched as Bright-Eagle strode purposefully towards the ceremonial fire and his waiting father. I now recognised the young woman who was with him. It was Wind-in-Her-Hair, daughter of Bear-Heart from the Forest of Rain. So, finally, all Bear-Heart's plans were coming to fruition and each tribe's special gifts would be united if these two married.

I was about to turn away and leave them to their privacy, when I saw a most unusual thing. Eye-of-the-Sun reached out and clasped his son's hand and drew him into an embrace. These really were changing times.

ACT 3, SCENE 5

ANDREW BEGINS TO SEE

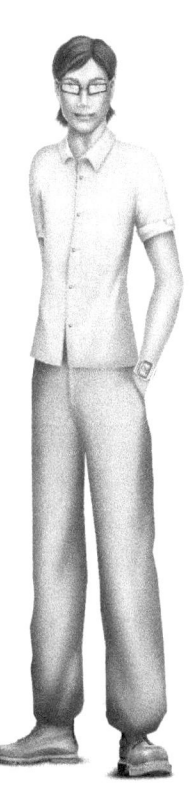

I woke refreshed even though we had slept on the ground on a bed of bracken. I hadn't had such a good night's sleep in ages. Maybe it was the lack of incidental lighting that is always present at home or perhaps it was because I didn't have as many thoughts running around in my brain.

Javier was nowhere to be seen, so I stretched and emerged from under the exquisitely woven blanket.

I hadn't seen it in the dark last night but now, even I could see, that it was truly a piece of art. I was just beginning to wonder if I could buy one when I remembered I was a scientist and not a tourist.

Even though it was early, everyone seemed to be up and it was already hot. I was so glad that we weren't still in the middle of the desert. There must have been a natural spring somewhere nearby, as there were a number of trees that created shade for the village and a small oasis but no running water.

I was looking around, relatively lost, when all of a sudden this woman started walking towards me. Javier was pacing beside her like a stalking panther. It was the woman who ran past us the night before. She was easy to recognise because she was so completely different from anyone else in the tribe, both in body shape and facial structure. Now that I could see her in the light, she took my breath away. She was extraordinarily beautiful. Her huge liquid brown eyes would have taken up all my attention, except for her mouth. Her lips were so full they were almost bursting. Then she smiled. I could literally feel myself go weak at the knees. I had always thought that kind of stuff was Hollywood rubbish but I can now attest to the fact that it really does happen.

She thrust out her hand. For a moment I felt bewildered. What was I meant to do? Just before I made a complete and utter idiot of myself my brain clicked into gear, and I put my hand out to shake hers. As if that wasn't enough, she started speaking. It must have been in her own tongue because it sounded completely different from the language that Javier and the guy at the fire were speaking the night before. If you can imagine a language that was like someone speaking a cross between Irish and French while eating a mango dipped in chocolate, then you would have some idea of the sound. It was succulent. I wouldn't normally describe something like that – it's a bit poetic for me – but honestly, I felt inspired. Then Javier was translating.

"Welcome, Andrew. We wish to embrace you into the heart of our tribe and hold you close in our arms. My father, Bear-Heart, has been waiting for you. He will be so overjoyed that you have finally arrived here safely and will take you into his bosom, like a son. My name is Wind-in-Her-Hair." Javier finished translating and raised an ironic eyebrow.

I just stood there dumbly staring at her, thinking about being embraced into her heart, until Javier cleared his throat. "Um, thank you. I am very pleased to meet you. My name is Andrew," I finally managed.

Oops. I looked at Javier, hoping he wouldn't translate that properly, considering she obviously knew my name. Why, just when you want to impress someone, does your brain turn to mush? But she graciously ignored my distractions except for a hint of a smile.

"I will be your companion as we walk together in harmony to the Forest of Rain. You can then meet our adored father, Bear-Heart. Bright-Eagle, the love of my life and the fullness of my heart, will also accompany us."

Just at that moment, Bright-Eagle appeared at her side. He smiled down at her and their eyes locked for a brief intimate moment. Then he turned his attention to me. He studied me for a moment, like I was some kind of stick insect, and then his eyes hardened. Well that was one piece of language I did understand, "Stay away from my girl!!!!!!"

I suppose it didn't help that I had been making googly eyes at the love of his life and that I still had my mouth open. I closed my mouth and swallowed. This was going to be one hell of a trip. And I thought the ride here had been bad . . .

ACT 3, SCENE 6

JAVIER AND THE BRITTLE FOREST

Well, apart from Andrew making a complete and utter fool of himself, everything was back on track. It was a day and half hike to the Forest of Rain. Bright-Eagle spent most of his time ensuring that he remained between Wind-in-Her-Hair and Andrew, which made any flow of conversation difficult. At night Wind-in-Her-Hair sang to the stars. The sound was melodious and hypnotic and we all fell into a deep and grateful sleep.

Even though I had been to the Forest of Rain hundreds of times, I was always amazed at how suddenly the forest appears. There is almost a line between the desert and the trees. Must be something to do with the soil, I suppose. Maybe that's something Andrew actually knows.

I was just about to ask him when it hit me just how sad the forest was. I could feel it physically; a pain like grief in my body. Even in the six months I had been away, the forest had deteriorated significantly. Many of the large trees were still alive, but all of the smaller shrubbery had died and the grasses, flowers and mosses had shrivelled into brittle corpses. It was heartbreaking.

I remembered coming here when dewdrops kissed every leaf and the cushions of moss seemed fit for dwarf thrones. Leaves had rustled everywhere with the movement of birds and tiny mammals. Coloured lichen had swung from trees like Christmas decorations and every branch sparkled with spiderwebs laced with water. When the sun shone through the trees, the forest literally glistened in an array of green light. Now the forest had the silence of a graveyard, and there were gaping holes in the canopy where dying trees had lost their leaves or fallen.

"My goodness, there mustn't have been rain for months," commented Andrew, shocked.

"It's been years. The villagers hand watered as much as they could but even the glacial stream has dried up," I replied.

"Why did Bear-Heart wait so long to get someone in here?"

"He didn't. The scientists he invited were all employed by the government. The government doesn't want to know. Under the forest are rich mineral reserves as well as the kinds of crystals that New Age people like to collect. Both are lucrative. If the people leave the Forest of Rain, mining can begin. At the moment, there is a court injunction that prevents that from happening."

"I can't believe it. You mean the government wants the forest to die."

"You are young in the ways of the world. All the villagers here hold onto the land by a tiny thread. That thread protects the land and it also protects the unique wisdom and understanding of these people. There is old magic in this place and once the village is deserted, that too will be lost."

Andrew was silent. I think he was finally feeling that this expedition was more than a big adventure, that he could go home and impress his friends with.

ACT 3, SCENE 7

ANDREW STARTS TO FEEL

Alright, I admit it; I have spent most of my life inside my head. I was always good at mathematics and science. The only literature I read was Sci Fi and, as a kid, *Dungeons & Dragons*. I could never really understand why people would want to talk about their emotions. You can't do anything about them anyway. Well, that's what I used to think. I'd rather rationalise a problem and get on with the solution or forget about it. Wallowing in emotions just seemed self-indulgent.

Now emotions seemed to be taking their revenge and I had absolutely no tools to deal with them. First, there was the carnal lust I was feeling for Wind-in-Her-Hair. My body was just going bananas and I couldn't seem to control it. It was unbelievably embarrassing. No wonder Bright-Eagle was keeping an eye on me. I couldn't blame him but I felt like a sparrow being watched by an eagle (no pun intended). Nobody had ever observed me like that and I felt that he could see inside my mind. It was very exposing. I couldn't hide.

Then last night when she started to sing, all the feelings that had been centred in other areas of my body rose up and concentrated in my heart. It was really painful and I had heaps of trouble sleeping. In the morning, I saw Wind-in-Her-Hair and Bright-Eagle in a private moment together. They were holding hands and looking deeply into each other's eyes, like some kind of religious ritual. I felt this jealous rage rip through me which was almost uncontrollable. I had to get away and went for a run. By the time I came back, they were all waiting for me. My embarrassment stepped up a notch to humiliation.

Now, I was walking through this forest that was clearly dying. In the past, rainfall had always been a statistic. I knew farmers had problems during droughts. I even had statistics on rates of depression and suicide. Instead of feeling any emotion, I had had an intellectual response, something like, "What a waste!" How does that happen? How do we become so detached from empathy and compassion? I looked back on my work and wondered if I had even been human.

Now everything was different. I suppose this was what people meant when they said they were 'emotionally connected'. Now I was feeling emotions for a forest. It was a kind of grief and I felt profoundly moved. I wanted to do whatever I could – but what was I going to be able to do? The problem seemed so huge. It was overwhelming and I felt powerless.

ACT 3, SCENE 8

JAVIER FEELS THE HEARTBEAT OF THE FOREST FADE

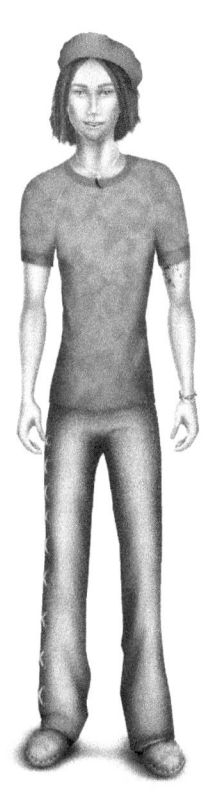

We heard the slow beat of drums long before we saw anyone. They beat like the dying heart of the forest. It was a sad lament; I had never heard it before. Usually the Tribe-that-Moves-and-is-Touched played their drums insistently like an expectant pulse. Now even the drums were fading.

We reached the village by mid-morning. The place was deserted apart from Bear-Heart and the drummer sitting by the fire. Bear-Heart seemed deep in meditation but Wind-in-Her-Hair approached him immediately. She knelt down behind him and wrapped her arms around his chest. They spent a few moments silently rocking. I sat down beside them and could feel the emotion welling up inside me in response to their unhidden vulnerability. Then he turned and took her face in his hands and wiped the tears from her eyes and brushed the hair back from her face, as you might a child. She smiled at him despite the sadness.

"So you are betrothed?" Bear-Heart asked, as if he already knew. She replied, "You feel it, Father?"

"I can feel your core joy despite the sadness, my sweet one. This is Bright-Eagle then." Bear-Heart stood up and opened his arms to the younger man. There was a moment's hesitation before Bright-Eagle melted into the older man's arms, as if he had been searching for them all his life.

Then he turned towards Andrew and me: "You are most welcome, Javier. It warms my heart that you and Andrew have finally arrived."

We hugged, as was the custom. When we finished, Bear-Heart turned and grasped hands with Andrew and drew him also into an embrace. Andrew accepted the embrace rather awkwardly at first before relaxing. They stood like that for a long time, longer than was custom even in this tribe. When they parted I could see Andrew's eyes swimming with unshed tears.

"Father, what has happened?" Wind-in-Her-Hair was the first to speak.

"My darling, as you know, the forest has been fading for a long time, but now it can no longer support our people. The last stream has completely dried. There is no water left. Yesterday we finished moving the families higher up into the mountains to where the glacial streams still flow. We will have to become a mountain people in order to survive. Our link to Mother-Forest will fade and Father-Mountain looms cold and stark."

"Is there nothing that can be done?" I asked.

"Nothing that I know of. I hope Andrew will tell his people before it is too late even for the mountains," replied Bear-Heart. "I will stay behind with the drummer until Andrew has finished his research. At least then the trees will know that we desert them reluctantly."

ACT 3, SCENE 9

ANDREW OVERFLOWS

I was completely overwhelmed with a deep shame. I could feel it welling up inside me and I was finding it hard to breathe.

There was something about this proud man's vulnerability and compassion that was ripping me open. He was everything I had wished my own father could be; strong, open, loving and completely connected. He was so honest about who he was and what he was feeling even if, like now, he was in terrible pain.

I thought about all the thoughtless things I did at home every day that led to the heating up of the planet. Driving the car instead of walking or taking the bus. The hundreds of drink bottles I bought rather than just refilling the same one. Everything I ate that wasn't organic. The general need to consume – all the things I felt I needed and wanted. The latest phone or computer. Even the crystals I bought for one of my girlfriends who had been a bit into New Age stuff must have been mined.

All of it, in one way or another, was contributing to the death of the forest. The mountain glaciers were receding, melting too quickly and now there was not enough left to sustain the streams in the forest. How easily I would have traded everything I had, just to see the water flowing here once more. 'Global Warming' – I had even been bored with the whole concept and all the hype, but now I was seeing the consequences up close and personal. It was incredibly painful.

Suddenly, my mind was in overdrive: there must be underground water. Surely that could be pumped up and into the forest. Maybe there was some way to make it rain. I had seen something on the net about making it rain in the desert – I had been really skeptical but it was worth a try. Maybe we could get a pipeline from up where the glacier still was and pump the water down. Maybe then it wouldn't disappear before it reached the forest. Um, maybe we could get the army to water-bomb the forest like they do during bush fires. Maybe we could raise money by mining a bit of land somewhere that no one uses and then we could afford to pay for a pipeline. Maybe, maybe, maybe we could . . .

I was babbling. I couldn't remember when my thoughts had become spoken words. They seemed to have been tumbling out of my mouth and now I just couldn't shut up about all the ways I could fix things so that the people could come back to the forest. All the ways I could make it up to these people. All the ways I could heal my own shame.

Bear-Heart listened politely as Javier impatiently translated and Bright-Eagle glared at me.

Finally, Bright-Eagle could bear it no longer and Javier translated. "So you think you can heal it, do you? With your bore water and your pipes and your mines. Do you feel nothing? Are you touched by nothing? What do you feel a mine would do to the heart of these people? You think the spirit of the land can be divided? That part of spirit doesn't matter but this does? For all your tears, do you still feel nothing? Are you so disconnected? That's the problem though, isn't it? You cannot feel because you live in your head."

For a moment, I could see the earth as Bright-Eagle did. One living breathing entity – Mother. Mother . . . I hadn't thought about her for a very long time, but now I had vivid pictures of her last days in the hospital dying of cancer. I had been in the doorway about to enter her room but I could see my Mum and Dad were having a private moment. So I paused and just watched, transfixed as my mother reached out her hand to my Dad and in a voice I could barely hear said:

"David, don't let them cut me open again. It's enough. And I want to stop the chemotherapy too. Really there is nothing they can do."

But Dad couldn't let it go: "Jane, you must. The doctors think you should. You're in their hands now."

Mum had smiled at him bravely, patted his hand and nodded. Then she looked up and smiled at me in the doorway. It was the last time I saw my mother. She had died on the operating table. I had always wondered what would have happened if she had never been operated on, never had chemo, how long she would have lived. Could it possibly have been any worse than what happened? It was just so typical of Dad; always having to follow the rules, listen to the experts, do what the doctors said . . .

Bear-Heart interrupted my thoughts and Javier translated for me:

"Andrew, for thousands of years we have felt the flow of water underneath the ground. If we redirect water from the last remaining glacial stream, then Bright-Eagle's tribe will have no oasis and the Tribe-that-Listens-and-Sings in Echo Canyon will stop having a stream through their lands.

When we interfere with nature, another part of nature feels the consequences. We also feel the heart of the miners and know we cannot trust them, nor can we trust the engineers who work beside them. They care only for themselves and their families, and not for the earth as a whole.

We cannot introduce anything artificial from the outside world, such as pipes, as that would simply scar Mother Earth more. We need to find a way to reach the Tribe-that-Thinks-and-Calculates. We want them to understand the truth that lies beyond logic and mere calculations, so that they can feel what is happening to the earth.

There is nothing more we can do for our forest home. The big trees will live on and maybe there will be some long-awaited rain. We will continue to water them as we can in a way that is in harmony with the flow of water in the underground streams. However, the rest of the forest has died and there is little we can do about it without the seasonal rains. We have helped as many of the animals as we can to move further up. It is of course most difficult for them to adapt.

I remember what the forest was like when I was a child, teeming with life and brimming with joy. So now, as I said, we must do what we can to reach your tribe before it is too late for the rest of the earth. He paused and then turned to his daughter and her betrothed. "Wind-in-Her-Hair and Bright-Eagle, do you have plans for your wedding?"

"Not yet," answered Wind-in-Her-Hair a little shyly.

"But, I'd like it to be soon as possible," added Bright-Eagle, smiling at Wind-in-Her-Hair despite everything.

"Would you mind if your wedding became a Gathering-of-the-Tribes to celebrate your union and also to talk more on these matters that stretch our heart?" Bear-Heart asked.

"Of course we wouldn't mind, Father," answered Wind-in-Her-Hair as she looked at Bright-Eagle for confirmation. He smiled at her. "We would be willing to do anything to help the forest."

"We will only have room for a gathering of that size here in the forest but it will be easier to make room for the guests now that the village has been moved. Are you sure it will be in harmony with your desires?"

"Father, it would be our greatest wedding gift," Wind-in-Her-Hair answered taking her father's hand and smiling.

ACT 3, SCENE 10

JAVIER AND THE WEDDING

Over the next weeks, there was a great deal of movement as the Forest People prepared for the wedding and guests began to arrive. Bear-Heart had sent invitations to the Tribe-that-Listens-and-Sings in Echo Canyon and to the Tribe-that-Sees-and-has-Visions. I myself was sent back to the cities to find and invite all those scientists and anthropologists who had visited him through the years. He even invited the guy who had become that spiritual teacher. I don't know where Bear-Heart got the patience.

"I know how you feel, Javier," he once said, catching me off guard. Of course, I had never said anything about how I felt. "But you know we need to open up channels of communication now between us and the Tribe-that-Thinks-and-Calculates."

I suppose I am a cynical man but there was one final stroke of Bear-Heart's plan that was tearing me apart. He wanted to invite a film crew to the wedding. When he told me, I could hardly speak – my jaw just dropped open.

"What?" I answered. I couldn't even be polite.

"Javier, don't say anything to anyone yet. I will have to connect with the other tribes and work with how they feel. It's just that I can't grasp another way to reach the Tribe-that-Thinks-and-Calculates."

"What makes you feel that film will?" I asked incredulous.

"We once had a director come here doing research for a film. He wanted to get in touch with how we lived. He put a canvas between two trees and projected images of other tribes onto the surface; it was fascinating, like a shadow play but more defined. In the end he said there was no point in making a film about us because there was no drama, no tragedy to make the film interesting. He said our tribe was 'too happy'."

"Typical," I murmured under my breath, shaking my head at the irony.

"You know, Javier, I feel we have that sadness now, that tragedy. I want him to record the wedding and then the forest dying."

"But you can't." Oh no, now I was telling the Chief what he could and couldn't do with his own tribe. But I couldn't help myself. "You do that and before you know it the whole place will be swarming with tourists. You might as well just kill your culture here right now."

Water off a duck's back – that is an expression that really describes the way Bear-Heart reacts to just about everything. Even though he felt things so deeply, he was rarely offended because he understood others so profoundly. Yet if he needed to, Bear-Heart could put you in your place with just a touch on your shoulder. That is what he did right at that moment.

"Javier," he said smiling at me, "I know you love us and wish to protect us, but there are things right now that are more important than our culture, even more important than our tribe's survival. Besides, having to move from the forest to the mountains has already impacted our culture. What haunts me is that if our forest is dying, if the glaciers are receding to a point that they never have before in our long history on these lands, what must be happening to the earth as a whole? There has been something seriously out of balance for years but now it is reaching a tipping point. I can feel it. We must do something radical."

"But Bear-Heart, how will filming the wedding help? How do you think Bright-Eagle and his father will feel about that?"

"Much the same as you do, I suppose," he said smiling, "but Javier I feel that a film about a wedding and love in the midst of a forest that is dying will be of interest to the Tribe-that-Thinks-and-Calculates, don't you? It will be a way of communicating our pain and may touch thousands of people. Isn't that so?"

I had to hand it to him. For a man who feels, he sure knew how to think.

He once told me that when he met someone new, he would send a part of his soul out to touch theirs. During this process, he could absorb a great deal about what drove their behaviour and how they felt. Maybe that was another reason he wanted Andrew close by, so he could get a further understanding of the Tribe-that-Thinks-and-Calculates. The interesting thing was that he did all this without manipulation. His sole motivation was love, and if people disagreed strongly enough, Bear-Heart was equally capable of surrendering and taking responsibility for any repercussions. This time, however, it seemed that he felt his mission was so important that he was going to engage that odd stubbornness that he adopted when he said the Great Spirit entered his body and he must follow the inner teacher.

But the risk seemed immense. To me the people were the most important thing, but for Bear-Heart and his tribe, their most sacred task was to serve Mother Earth and Father Sky.

"Who knows, Javier. With the collective wisdom of all the tribes we may come up with a better solution," Bear-Heart said quietly. "I just can't feel a better one at the moment and we must start somewhere."

Maybe Bear-Heart wasn't so certain after all. Anyway, I would do anything to find a way to protect these people and I'm sure Bear-Heart would too. It's just that his agenda was bigger than mine.

ACT 3, SCENE 11

ANDREW LEARNS TO SPEAK FROM THE HEART

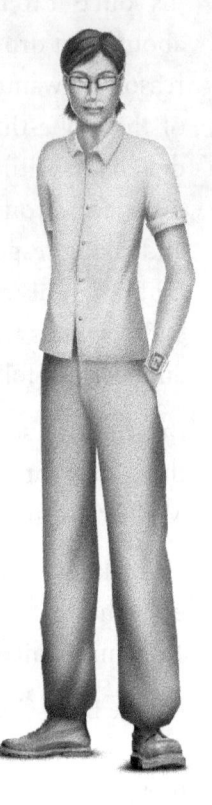

It had been months now since I had come to the Forest of Rain and I had picked up quite a bit of the language, not because I was very good at languages, but because I was so determined. My accent must have sounded horrendous but at least I could be understood. There was also the added benefit of the fact that Wind-in-Her-Hair, despite the preparations for her wedding, had taken it upon herself to teach me.

She also wanted to learn my language. She said: "Some day I hope, in the very distant future, I will be head of this tribe and I'll need to be able to communicate with the Tribe-that-Thinks-and-Calculates."

That was a sad truth. No doubt there would be more of us coming to the forest at some time. I would rather keep these people all to myself but that was as unlikely as it was selfish. I was still as tormented by Wind-in-Her-Hair's physical presence as I was addicted to it. Much to Bright-Eagle's chagrin, we actually spent quite a bit of time together. I have never really felt so completely out of control. I had so many conflicting emotions.

My jealousy of Bright-Eagle was really eating me up and making me irritable. Despite the seriousness of the situation with the forest and Bear-Heart's preparations to 'touch the world', as he put it, I knew the chief could feel it. Once, in the middle of everything he was doing, he put his big hand on my shoulder and quietly said: "There will be one for you, my surrogate son."

The other thing that was driving me crazy was the way people made decisions here. It all seemed so slow to me, with endless meetings, where everyone sat in a circle and had their say. I would just sit and listen; I didn't think it was my place to speak. After all, this was their home not mine, and besides, I felt so ashamed. I knew that it was through the thoughtless actions of my tribe that this beautiful land was being destroyed.

The meetings were getting larger by the day as more and more people began to gather for the wedding. It was consensus decision-making on a scale I had never seen before. Even Bear-Heart had to plead his case to the rest of the tribes. He couldn't just tell them what he wanted them to do; he had to inspire them to agree with him. It reminded me a bit of Ancient Greece except no-one voted. Everyone had to agree. It was more democratic than democracy. It was pretty incredible.

Bear-Heart was a tremendous orator; it was like he could speak to everyone's concerns before they voiced them. I wondered how he did that and asked him.

"Can you feel the wind through the trees, Andrew?" Bear-Heart asked in response. A question from left field as usual.

"Yes, of course."

"The tribes' emotions are like a gust of wind and the individual concerns are like the leaves swirling within it. I can feel the leaves that come my way, catch them and address each one.

The wind itself also has a feeling, sometimes cold, sometimes warm or even hot. This is the collective emotion of the group."

I just stood there listening to what seemed incomprehensible to me. Then he said something I totally didn't understand:

"When I breathe in this wind, I can feel the Great Spirit speak to me through the collective emotions of the tribe and I simply say what the Spirit prompts me to."

Well, that's what it sounded like. I could have got it totally wrong because it just didn't make any sense, but then nothing much made sense.

"Andrew, I'd like you to speak at the Gathering-of-the-Tribes," Bear-Heart interrupted my thoughts. "Me?" I answered bewildered. "Why would you like me to speak? This is your gathering. Besides, I wouldn't know what to say. To be honest, I'm pretty hopeless at public speaking unless of course you want to be bored to death." I managed a weak smile.

"There will be quite a few people from the Tribe-that-Thinks-and-Calculates and I feel it would help them if they received a summary of the facts. Anyway, think about it," Bear-Heart said smiling and using one of my own turns of phrase.

I felt both incredibly humbled by the invitation and terrified that I would look like an idiot in front of the dignified tribal people. I had spent long enough in the Tribe-that-Moves-and-is-Touched to know that it was important to speak about my feelings, particularly if they were negative. So the moment I found Bear-Heart alone again, I basically told him that I was scared.

His advice was, "Speak from the heart."

I didn't find that advice very helpful. "What if I can't remember all the information? How is my heart going to help me there?"

"Trust the soul of the women inside you."

Now I really had no idea what he was talking about. I wondered if that was similar to Jungian Psychology – the anima or animus – but I couldn't remember which was which.

Bear-Heart smiled. "Whether we are male or female there is a part of us that is linked to the Great-Feminine. She is the keeper of all our memories, imagination and creativity. The best way to prepare for an important speech is to go inside and let her know what you want her to create. Then simply wait. She will, when she is ready, start giving you the answers you seek."

"But Bear-Heart, how do I do that? What do I do? Just close my eyes and think in my head: 'Hey Great-Feminine, give me the words'?"

"Well . . ." Bear-Heart smiled. I did get the feeling that he found me endlessly amusing but I never felt judged. It was like his amusement helped me to laugh at myself.

"When we are children, we are encouraged to get a feeling that the Great-Feminine is sitting beside us and to speak with her like we would with our mother or girlfriend. I am sure you understand, very respectfully. Then you let her gather the information for you. She may direct you to speak to certain people, seek something new, or in your case, go over your scientific data. You let her guide you to what you need. It would be the same process if you were a woman. Like I said, we have both the feminine and masculine energies inside of us since it takes both a woman and a man to create us."

"So what happens then? Do I just wait?" This was so different from how I'd been taught at school. At school writing anything had seem like a push, something you had to discipline or force yourself to do. Waiting for a part of you to give you the answer would have been labelled procrastination or laziness.

"Yes, that's right. You wait. When she is ready, she will start to speak to you and give you the words. After that, but not before, you can use the logical part of your mind to find the best structure for the speech so that others will understand. When you have done all of that, put the speech into your body."

"Put the speech into my body?" I asked even more puzzled.

"Yes, say it over and over again, as if you were delivering it to the gathering."

I realised that what he meant was to rehearse the speech out loud and engage what athletes call 'body memory'. Normally, I would have spent hours and hours writing the speech but I would never rehearse it. I would have just relied on reading my notes.

So I followed his advice. After all, I had nothing to lose. Nothing could be worse than the way I felt about speech-giving anyway. I let the Great-Feminine know that I wanted to create a speech about the forest and what my research had revealed. I also asked if she could give me a speech that was moving, insightful and suited my audience. I thought it would be good protocol to say that I was also open to her ideas or anything the Great Spirit might like me to say as well.

She didn't seem to want me to do any more research. I suppose that was because I had already spent months gathering data and speaking with the various tribes. So I felt like I was just hanging around waiting and waiting.

It occurred to me that it was a bit like taking a girl you really liked on a date and you get to the door and she says: "Hang on, I'm not quite ready yet." So you just sit in the lounge room waiting for her. Bear-Heart smiled when I told him this. I wasn't sure if he would understand what I meant but perhaps the concept was universal.

"Women in our tribe don't take long to get ready. They are too impatient," he said, "but my brother married a woman from the Tribe-that-Sees-and-has-

Visions and he is always complaining about how long she takes to get dressed. In this suitaition you're off the hook, Andrew, because you don't have to sit and wait. You can get on with other things."

I found this a bit tricky. It was like I wanted to keep peeking into the room to see if she was ready. Bear-Heart laughed and laughed when I told him that. He said that I was being a little bit rude and not treating the Great-Feminine with trust and respect. It was important for me to bide my time and leave her alone.

So I waited what seemed like an age, even though it was only a few days. The preparations for the Gathering-of-the-Tribes seemed to be ramping up and I felt like the date for my speech was coming soon and this made me very nervous.

Then one day I took a hike up to the glacial stream in the mountains where it was still visible. I sat down and became lost in the water flowing over the rocks and suddenly my speech started flowing as well. I started to say it out loud. When I had finished, I realised there were things I would like to rearrange, information or content I wanted to put in a different, more logical order. This I did and then started saying the speech again. I kept saying it out aloud until I felt it was complete and in the best structure so that others would understand.

I was so excited and couldn't wait to tell Bear-Heart. As usual he smiled and then put a spanner in my works.

"Now, my surrogate son, before you stand up and speak at the Gathering, you must let it all go and speak from the heart."

I couldn't believe it. After all that. All I wanted to do was hang onto it, like I once would have hung onto my notes.

Bear-Heart put his hand on my shoulder and said: "Before you speak, let it go. Trust the Great-Feminine will be there when you need her. She doesn't break her 'dates'." He said the last word in my language and then walked off with an amused laugh.

ACT 3, SCENE 12

JAVIER AND HIS LITTLE SISTER JENNY

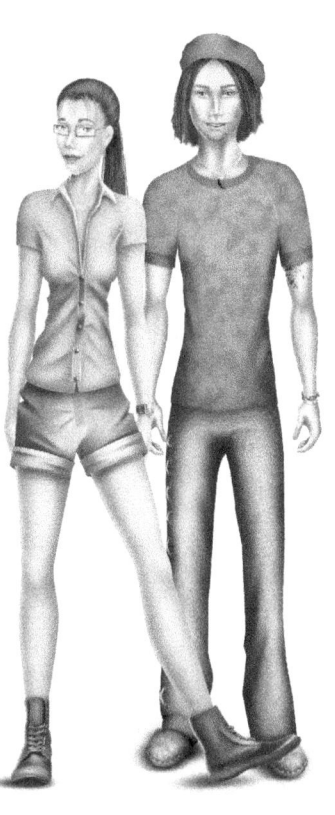

Even my sister, Jenny, had been invited to the Gathering. Bear-Heart was going all out. He said that maybe she could be a bridge between his tribe and the Tribe-that-Thinks-and-Calculates. She arrived in the middle of the night. She had caught the last plane into the region and she and some other scientists had spent hours driving to the Forest of Rain. I suppose we will have to stop calling it that soon, since there is no rain.

My little sister was really different from me. She didnt grow up with the tribes of this region and never learned their languages. She was educated in the city and I found her kind of annoying because she was really more like the Tribe-that-Thinks-and-Calculates than they were. I suppose she tried really hard to fit in, whereas I knew I could never fit in, so I never bothered to try.

We probably could have looked alike if she was more in touch with her body and senses, but she spent most of her time in her head. In fact Andrew reminded me a lot of her in his attitude to life, even though he was really making a huge effort to change. I suppose Wind-in-Her-Hair's attention would have that affect on just about anyone.

When Jenny arrived, Andrew and Wind-in-Her-Hair rose from the fire and greeted her. Andrew seemed pretty excited to be able to speak his own language with someone who was a native speaker. So it was a moment before Jenny saw me. When she did, she smiled shyly. We hadn't always been on the best of terms and she was never quite sure how I would react. I smiled reassuringly and went towards her and put my arms around her: "So, little sister, you decided to come and rough it, did you? How are your film studies going?"

She gave me her awkward hug back. "You're a bit behind the times. I'm studying anthropology now." I gave a little internal groan. Not another one.

With unusual perception she said: "Don't be like that. We can't all be purely subjective like yourself." Then she playfully punched me on the arm.

I suppose she was all grown up after all, even if she was my little sister. "I think you have met everyone."

"Yes, I introduced myself since you didn't bother getting up to greet me!" Jenny gave me a mock 'telling off' look. Actually it made her look a lot like her mother but I didn't say anything.

Wind-in-Her-Hair smiled and then said: "You are most welcome here Jenny. Would you like to come to the women's tent and put down your things? It's this way."

It was quite bizarre to hear Wind-in-Her-Hair speak Andrew's language. She made it sound quite beautiful, even if the words themselves were devoid of emotion. The way she rounded and elongated the vowels made it sound like edible pieces of art.

ACT 3, SCENE 13

ANDREW OBSERVES JAVIER AND THE TRIBES

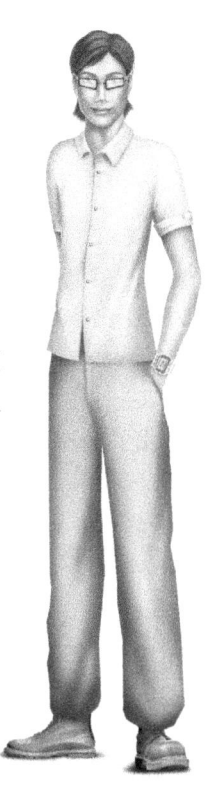

It was weird to think of Jenny as Javier's sister. To be honest I was a bit intimidated by him. He had the all-masculine good looks and charisma of a rock star and he was smart and yes, incredibly gifted too. It was like he had the qualities of all the tribes mixed together and he could draw on them at will. The more people from each of the tribes turned up, the more I could see the individual qualities of each and how easily Javier could adapt his language and behaviour to suit them.

When Bright-Eagle's tribe gathered from the Painted Desert, I found I could observe things that I had missed when I first met them. I suppose back then I had been too caught up in my head to notice much outside myself. Of course I had seen that they were visually striking, with their tall slender bodies, angular faces and gorgeous clothes. But now I noticed more details, such as their unbelievably high cheekbones that defined the lean shape of their faces and their impossibly shiny hair. How did they do that? Even with commercial shampoos and heaps of water, my hair lay lank and lifeless kind of sticking to my forehead. Not that I had ever much cared before but now I couldn't help comparing my appearance and finding it incredibly lacking.

Then there was the exquisitely-coloured beading and woven cloth that all their clothes were made from. They were as striking as a peacock's feathers without being gaudy; everything they wore was tasteful and dignified. More than all of this, however, it was their bearing that really held them apart. It was like they had a perfect image of who they were and where they fitted into the picture.

I found them pretty daunting, if truth be told. I felt like I should be straightening my hair or brushing down my clothes.

Javier had no such problem. You would see him talking to their chief, Eye-of-the-Son, as if he was a chief himself. It was kind of uncanny because when Javier spoke with them, particularly in their language, he looked completely different. His posture was very straight and he even looked taller. His movements and speech were much faster and everything was more direct – kind of like a bird of prey. Anyway, he was definitely like another person.

Wind-in-Her-Hair's mother's tribe was also gathering from Echo Canyon. They were the Tribe-that-Listens-and-Sings and were often found in a circle, talking, singing and harmonising together. I even came across them in little circles surrounding the trees and, well I think they were singing to them. It was kind of like tree hugging except with sound. Their language was very unusual; it was like a collection of symbolic nature sounds. Wind-in-Her-Hair told me the words for speech, voice, tone etc were all bird noises, while the word for pleasure was the sound of a purring cat, and words for wind or flowing water all sounded like the real thing. This might seem odd when described but it was actually very beautiful and the speech had a variety of rhythms that reflected mood and many different tones almost like a song.

Physically, they were somewhere in between the round voluptuousness of the Tribe-that-Moves-and-is-Touched and the straight up and down of the Tribe-that-Sees-and-has-Visions. They had a beauty all of their own. It wasn't earthy and tactile or visually striking – it had an 'other worldly' quality. Just as sound doesn't quite have a physical presence because you can't touch it or see it. What you did sense was that they were constantly listening, either to their own internal voice, what others were saying or the subtle remaining sounds of the forest. I suppose that's where the tribe's name came from: the Tribe-that-Listens-and-Sings.

I would come across Javier sitting in a circle with this tribe and if I hadn't honed my observation skills, I would have completely missed him. All that masculine charisma disappeared as he blended in with the tribe, just like certain instruments blend together in an orchestra until you can hardly tell one instrument from another.

Every now and then he might do a 'little solo piece' when he wanted to ask a question and then he would merge back in as he listened. I was astounded. He was unrecognisable.

There was great rejoicing when this tribe first started to turn up because it had been a long time since they had seen Wind-in-Her-Hair. One of the very last people to arrive was the Chieftess, Wind-in-Her-Hair's grandmother, Crystal-Call. She was truly a magnificent woman. Even though she must have been very old, she had an ageless beauty like some kind of Moon Goddess. Her long pure white hair hung down her back and was tucked neatly behind her ears. Her eyes were inky-black and her skin was almost translucent. She was as cool as Wind-in-Her-Hair was warm. She stood straight but not rigid. Instead there was flexibility in her stance. It was as if she would flow with the wind. She had her head tilted a little to the side like she was permanently listening to the earth with one ear and the sky with the other, which I suppose she probably was. It was interesting to watch her because although she was obviously strong and sometimes formidable, there was that kind of transparency about her like she was an apparition from another world. She had the same ethereal quality as music.

They didn't touch when they met but rather embraced each other with sound by singing together. It was exquisitely beautiful and all the tribes gathered to listen to them being reunited. Crystal-Call had been married to the old Chief of the Tribe, Whispering-Spirit. He had done an unusual thing and abdicated his leadership in order to promote her as Chieftess. Apparently, he said that she was the natural leader and he was happy to take a secondary role. They had lived very happily together for many years until he had passed smiling in his sleep.

I think out of all the tribes, I loved watching Javier interact with the Tribe-that-Moves-and-is-Touched most of all. It was like watching an intimate dance, like some kind of very relaxed salsa. It was even better now that he didn't have to translate for me.

It was a bit weird watching him with Wind-in-Her-Hair. Their inter- actions were very touchy-feely, like a bear cub playing with a lion kitten. When he hugged her, he would lift her off the ground and swing her around. She would laugh, that great laugh of hers, one of complete abandon because no-one had ever told her she was too loud. Then there were hands lingering in each other's grasp, extended eye contact, a lingering kiss on the cheek with arms encircling each other's waists. It was pretty full on, if I thought about it in my own context, but in this tribe it was just standard practice.

I thought I would be jealous but I kind of knew it was just the customs of friendship here, so it never ate me up like her interactions with Bright-Eagle did. Now that was love. It was like some kind of invisible energy reached out and connected them whenever they were in close proximity. In fact one time when we were alone, Wind-in-Her-Hair told me that their tribe believed that everything you touch created an energy connection or cord between you and it. She said that it was through this connection and the transference of energy that you knew how someone was feeling.

"What do you feel happens to that connection when someone dies?" I wondered. I was kidding myself that it was an impersonal question.

"Who has passed that has caused you so much pain, Andrew? Is that why you push your feelings away?" she asked.

I wasn't quite sure what to say but I knew it was time to be honest.

"My mother. She died two years ago now, of cancer. Dad and I never spoke of it, so I didn't really know what to do with the feelings. I miss her so much." Strangely, I was still fighting with the feelings. I felt so vulnerable.

"Oh Andrew, I understand your pain. My mother has also passed." She reached out and cupped my face. My hands were shaking as I reached to touch her face as well.

All of my emotions broke through as I sobbed while looking deeply into her eyes and she cried too, completely open, completely vulnerable. We held each other's faces collecting the tears. After that we clasped our wet hands together and talked about our mothers. I suppose it was some kind of ritual here but that didn't matter to me; it was heart-wrenchingly tender.

When we finally fell silent, she very slowly kneeled in front of me then she took my face in both her hands and very deliberately and tenderly placed a kiss on each cheek where my tears were still wet. When she did, it was like her whole being was present in her lips and all her love passed into me. The two kisses were very conscious, slow and lingering.

It rocked my world.

I think it was the first time since my mother died that I felt truly loved and connected. I don't know how to describe it. I was touched, truly touched, and I felt that I would never feel lonely again. Afterwards, I felt a tremendous calm. Ever since I have been able to sit still and do nothing at all, perhaps for the first time in my life.

Even so, I was grateful Bright-Eagle didn't see us – I am not sure what he would have thought, but Javier did. When we had finished and Wind-in-Her-Hair left, he surprised me by putting his arm around my shoulders.

"You begin to open your heart, Andrew. It's a good thing; I feel the changes in you. You have received the Kiss of Friendship. In this tribe it is a bond for life. You're a lucky man. Very few people receive such a gift."

He gave my shoulder a squeeze and then walked off, throwing me a warm smile over his shoulder. I wasn't sure what to think. On the one hand, I felt a bit like I had been caught being overly intimate with someone else's betrothed. On the other, I felt that it was so important for me to start to feel and Wind-in-Her-Hair was definitely my catalyst. I didn't want to give that up. I couldn't work out whether that was selfish or not.

ACT 3, SCENE 14

JAVIER TRANSLATES FOR ANDREW AT THE GATHERING

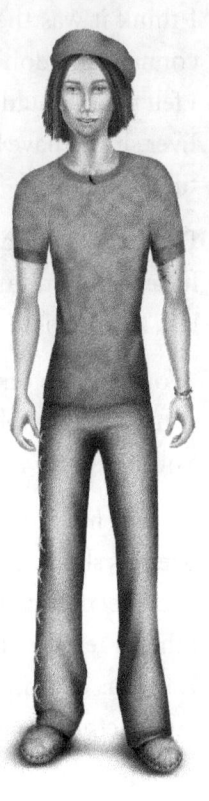

So finally all the members of each tribe had gathered, including the scientists and anthropologists from the Tribe-that-Thinks-and-Calculates. The three tribes of the region could all understand each other so I only had to translate Andrew's speech into the Tribe-that-Moves-and-is-Touched language.

Surprisingly, Bear-Heart asked the gathering if Andrew could speak first. In the months that he had been here, he had gathered a great deal of data. So when he spoke it was actually quite impressive. He talked about rates of rainfall in the forest and what had been happening recently. Then the importance of certain plant species that were unique to the area and would become extinct if the forest disappeared, and how certain animals depended on them for food.

Apparently there were also some unique medicinal herbs in the area; some had already been sent to research laboratories by previous scientists. One was a natural birth control plant which had no known side effects. In fact it was known to strengthen the body. It was how this tribe controlled their numbers so they could live in harmony with the resources nature had available and still be able to make love as much as they wanted. This, of course, was very important for the Tribe-that-Moves-and-is-Touched who made love often. The previous scientist had sent it to a laboratory where numerous tests had been done to verify the experience of the tribe but the company felt it would be too expensive to change all their manufacturing processes. They said they were perfectly happy with the profits they were making from the birth control pill they currently sold. I suppose it helped that they also sold medication to deal with the side effects, thereby doubling their profits. It sure was a cynical world.

Another herb had a major impact on the immune system and thyroid gland. Andrew pointed out that this was very significant in the world beyond the three tribes where obesity was often caused by undetected or sub-pathological hypothyroidism or underactive thyroid. This took some translating into tribal language however I did the best that I could. Everybody knew that when tribal people left their homes and lived in the city that they put on a lot of weight and obesity was a major problem. It was particularly prevalent for the Tribe-that-Moves-and-is-Touched but no one knew why. It turns out that one of the common herbs that all the tribes used to season food was high in iodine and that helped to regulate the thyroid. I found that pretty interesting and when I finally managed the translation everybody nodded. It was a great thing to know because they could then send that herb to their city cousins. Then Andrew paused and said with more heightened emotion:

"For me personally, the most important herbs are the ones known by the Tribe-that-Moves-and-is-Touched to heal breast cancer. I had extensive talks with a woman from the Tribe-who-Listens-and-Sings who had a strange, uneven lump in her breast. The tribe took the unprecedented decision to have her taken to the nearest hospital in the city. Javier accompanied her to translate. She had the tests done and it had come back positive and the cancer had spread and metasticised. She had been offered various treatments but decided to come home and consult the other tribes for possible cures."

Andrew then turned and smiled at the Chieftess of the Tribe-that-Listens-and-Sings.

"That woman was Crystal-Call and she has given me permission to tell her story."

Crystal-Call nodded and smiled at Andrew to continue. "Wind-in-Her-Hair, who is Crystal-Call's granddaughter, found a combination of herbs from the Forest of Rain and administered them to Crystal-Call both orally and through ingenious enemas over three months. After the first week, Crystal-Call was very sick with vomiting and diarrhoea. That was the first stage of healing. She went through many other stages that included shamanistic energy work by various other medicine people as well as continuing the herbal treatment. When she felt she was completely cured, she decided to go back to the hospital to show that other treatments were possible. They confirmed that she had indeed been cured, although they called it 'spontaneous remission'. They didn't want to know anything about what Crystal-Call had done or what medicine might be growing in the forest."

Then Andrew pulled a handful of various seeds from his pocket and held them in his trembling hand and tears glittered in his eyes reflecting the flames from the fire. He said:

"These little seeds could have saved my mother. The plants themselves are now dead from lack of water but Wind-in-Her-Hair and I have collected these seeds. She can still recognise the plants even when dead and knows the areas where they can be collected. If this extraordinary resource is in the forest, what else is still invisible to us? Wind-in-Her-Hair and I will collect as many of the seeds as possible and take them to the Seed Library in the capital but there is so much that could have been that is already lost."

He took a moment to gather himself, turning his head to shake the tears away.

"Bear-Heart is correct – the glaciers are receding and the lack of rain is in fact the result of the actions of the Tribe-that-Thinks-and-Calculates. Global warming is the result of air pollution and it affects the world as a whole. But even if the world was not heating up, pollution is at deadly levels in the waterways, in the oceans and in the sky, and this in turn affects all aspects of food production. At each stage, there are further chemical additives or leaching of chemicals from storage containers or production methods. This pollution affects the fertility of both animals and humans and increasingly, couples need fertility treatment to have babies, creating further chemical stress on both the mother and the child. Asthma, behavioural issues, learning problems, allergies and obesity are at an all-time high and for the first time life expectancy is going down in the cities. There is now a collection of first class scientific evidence proving that pollution and the proliferation of chemicals in our food chain significantly affects our health and the health of the world as a whole. I am truly ashamed of what my tribe has done to this forest, to Mother Earth and Father Sky."

He looked around the dozens of faces lit up by the firelight and held their gaze until I finished translating. Then he sadly shook his head and sat down. His speech was sensitive and yet scientific, not that the tribes needed anyone to tell them what was happening to the earth – they could feel it, hear it and see it for themselves – but it was a summary that made the scientific evidence clear.

It was interesting to hear the science of what we could sense. It was the first time I had an appreciation for objectivity. Obviously it was that very objectivity that allowed the Tribe-that-Thinks-and-Calculates to decimate and pollute the earth because they really saw themselves as separate from it. If they had a subjective experience of Mother Earth, they wouldn't be able to destroy her because they would feel her trauma inside their own bodies. Instead, this objective tribe was so disconnected they could impart centuries of pain on the earth and only future generations would really suffer. But the good thing about Andrew's objectivity was that, for his tribe, fact appeared to be something irrefutable and tangible. This was something they might finally take seriously.

Anyway, whatever the outcome, it was clear that Andrew had come a long way and was able to feel as well as, think. Bear-Heart must have been very proud. I looked over at him and he smiled and nodded at Andrew. Yes, he had been right in his understanding of Andrew and Andrew would surely become a tremendous advocate for our cause in his own tribe. Well, really it wasn't our cause. It was equally important for every tribe that inhabited the earth, including his own.

Crystal-Call was the next person to stand and speak. Her voice was a slow lament and the emotion could be heard even if one couldn't understand the symbols of the language.

"Last night I listened to a tree dying. The tree told me that her roots could not hear life in the soil and so she could not draw the vital melody into her branches to be expressed. She said she had sung on the earth for a thousand cycles and believed she would be here for a thousand more, but now she will become silent and the notes of her song will dissipate and die on the wind.

"I asked her if she could pause a while longer until I found some water to revitalise her melody but she said she was too weary to carry the tune and could bear the disharmony no longer. After a few moments she emitted a dry cracking sound and then was silent. I called to her and sang to her, my voice strangled with despair, but she was already gone and there was a great emptiness left in the Spirit Song where her voice had been."

She then turned to Andrew, her voice husky with grief.

"Can the Tribe-that-Thinks-and-Calculates hear nothing but what is going on inside their own heads? Can they not hear the holes of silence as the animals and plants die? How can they be so insensitive? I asked the Great Spirit and she said that your tribe does not know how to listen and therefore cannot hear. How can we get them to understand if they will not listen? Is there no way to speak to them, Andrew?"

Before Andrew could say anything, and to what seemed his great relief, Eye-of-the-Sun stood in all his glory. Tall, his long black hair streaked with grey, he was a most imposing figure. He seemed godlike and at this moment his eyes were blazing with a dark red fire.

"No, Crystal-Call. They cannot hear, nor can they see. With the visible evidence all around them of their stupidity, they still ignore their vision. Javier has told me how the Eye-of-the-Storm rips the coasts and destroys everything in its flood path, while in other places, dry cracks open the once fertile earth in jagged pieces like lightning bolts. Every year the earth heats up and they can measure the rising temperature with their science and still no one sees the catastrophe awaiting. We don't need their science to see that the snow on the Great Mountain recedes. This is not just in our land. It is all over Mother Earth. Yet their chiefs clash, closing their eyes to the truth. They only look with the eyes of greed and power and care nothing for what destruction they leave behind."

Then he turned to Bear-Heart.

"How many scientists have come here? How many engineers have wanted to rip our lands open to find what they call black gold, precious metals and crystals under the deserts and the forests? That is all they can picture. They see no beauty, they imagine no magic, they have no vision for the future. They are blind. How many times have they promised to do something different, take their message back to their tribe and make them see what is happening? And what has changed? Nothing! Why do you continue to befriend this tribe, Bear-Heart? I am blind to your purpose."

Bear-Heart rose in answer. "What you say is true, Eye-of-the-Sun, and Crystal-Call, your questions are valid and well considered.

"I, too, feel the pain of the earth. The death of each tree and animal adds to the grief in my body until I wonder how much dispair I can endure. When I was a child this forest was teeming with life and glistening with vitality. Now all is dried and shrivelled. My tribe has lost its home. We can no longer call this place the Forest of Rain because no rain has fallen for so many years.

"But if we close our ears, eyes and heart to the Tribe-that-Thinks-and-Calculates, how will they ever learn to feel? We must find a way to reach them that touches their hearts and inspires them to action. We must find a way to help them hear, see and feel. Otherwise it will not just be our forest that dies but everywhere will eventually be laid to waste and there will be no refuge in which to heal. What say you, visitors? What tools do you have in your world that would help people to listen, see and feel? What avenues are there to open communication so that the rest of your tribe can experience what you have tonight?"

It really had to be Jenny who would take such obviously laid bait. After all, she had majored in film before switching to anthropology and that was after she had left her science degree. She was the perpetual student. Whoever was her latest set of friends, that was her biggest influence. She would swap and change what she was studying depending on them. I suppose she really, really wanted to belong because she felt so lost. She was probably that bit too nerdy for the film gang, hence her move into anthropology.

Crystal-Call had once told me something very interesting. We were actually related to her. She told me that my grandmother was her cousin. When I told Jenny, she was over the moon. I suppose she felt that she finally had a tribe to which she belonged. Maybe that's what inspired her to take anthropology.

I don't know. I hadn't had much of a chance to speak with her because she was always hanging out with Andrew and Wind-in-Her-Hair. I suppose it was fair enough. It was pretty exciting for anyone to find out they were related to Wind-in-Her-Hair, however distant.

ACT 3, SCENE 15

ANDREW LISTENS TO JENNY

I had been listening to Javier translate. It was pretty interesting now that I could speak some of the language. There was quite a bit one had to interpret because there just weren't words in our language to describe it all. Then Jenny stood up. She looked a bit out of place like we all did, dressed in her khakis. I always wondered about that – why peace-loving people so often wore army clothes and colours. I suppose it was like saying even uniforms can be transformed. She looked radiant. I could see just a glimpse of her tribal ancestry in her cheeks as they glistened in the firelight. Then she spoke.

"Don't give up hope on us. Yes, we are the tribe that values thoughts and calculations more than anything else, however, we can also hear, see and feel. When you ask your questions, Crystal Call, they are the same questions I ask myself. When the fire lights up your eyes in righteous anger, Eye-of-the-Sun, my passion flares too. When your heart aches with pain, Bear-Heart, I feel myself cry.

"Most of the time, however, we do not notice our senses because our internal thoughts go round and round in circles of irrelevant detail, but when you speak, I am brought back into myself. I see that my small body is part of the earth as a whole and I realise how lonely and separate I have become.

"I know it's not apparent but we, like you, yearn for unity and know intuitively that we need to face our emotional pain. So we seek a way to understand. There is a medium we can use that allows us to hear, see and feel. It may seem odd that we need to sit in a darkened room and watch moving pictures on a wall to see the consequences of our actions but that is the best way. In the dark, we are not distracted by anything else and can focus for a short period of time.

I think we can use film and story to get your message across and touch the hearts of our tribe. After all, before we dwelt in the city, we too were part of the tribes." Bear-Heart stood and clapped.

"What say you?" he asked addressing the tribes.

Eye-of-the-Sun stood.

"Do you not see if we put the forest on film the Tribe-that-Thinks-and-Calculates will be arriving here by the busloads? First, there will be the tourists taking photos and objectifying our land and us. Then, there will be the scientists paid by mining companies to see if all the facts are true. Finally, the men in suits from the government will come. They will say: "Well, now that the land can no longer support the tribes, we might as well use it for mining," and they will justify it by saying that the money will help the tribes adjust to modern culture.

"Before we know it, the laws will be changed and all the land will be dug up. Gold will be sold, gems will be taken to adorn the hands of the rich and crystals will end up in New Age shops. When mining happens, there will be no hope for the forest and its legacy. There will be no hope for our people. The mines will attract hundreds from the city. They will bring their culture, their alcohol, their food and some young people from our tribes will be lured away as the polluted land, water and air no longer anchors them to Mother Earth.

"The film will be talked about for a while and then it will end up in some video store collecting dust and that will be all that is left of our tribal culture and lands. Just because I live in the tribes, do not think I have closed my eyes to this other tribe and their ways. My vision is strong and I see into the hearts and minds of men. Our young have been to the cities and come home to our way of life, as I did, because our tribal lands anchor our vision. We know what happens in the Tribe-that-Thinks-and-Calculates. Their minds are as inconsistent as clouds that drift across the sky. They promise one thing and do another as their mind changes with the wind."

Eye-of-the-Sun sat down to tremendous applause and nodding of heads. I wondered how Bear-Heart was going to deal with this one. But it was Wind-in-Her-Hair who stood and addressed the gathering.

"When my mother died, I felt as if my heart was wrenched from my chest. I felt

I would never recover. My father's grief was even greater and we reached out and cradled each other. We cried and spoke about her. I sang her songs and we visited her grave. I planted trees and her favourite herbs and flowers to keep her company. Butterflies would gather around the flowers and bees would sing their busy songs and finally, I found a sense of peace because life could go on.

"When Bright-Eagle and I fell in love, part of our souls' connection was the loss of our mothers. One of the many things we could share was our grief, as well as our laughter and happiness. We hope our love will bring fruitfulness and children will be born to continue the cycle. When Andrew came into our lives, it was the loss of his mother that brought about his ability to feel through pain. Through facing that pain, he found a gateway to truly connect with others.

"My mother's grave is one of the few places in the forest that still lives because, like other gravesites, it has been constantly watered, no matter how much effort was needed. If the forest dies completely and my mother's tree disappears, the miners and the government will come anyway and dig up this land.

"There won't be any tourists, they will not take their photographs, but my mother's grave will be dug up anyway. It is just that no one but us will know about it.

"When I see the forest of my ancestors die, my heart is wrenched from my chest all over again. I am a daughter of the forest and she is my mother. I climb the mountain slopes to the glacial streams and I water my mother's grave to keep a part of her alive in the trees and the herbs and flowers. In keeping her memory alive, I keep a part of Mother Forest alive too. But what will I do if all of Mother Earth dies? Then what? There will be no healing. Our spirits will be lost in the loneliness of space and our planet will become another empty rock, forever barren. No-one will sing the songs of our ancestors. No one will water the forest with tears of emotion and there will be no vision of the future. Andrew, what do you think?"

I felt Wind-in-Her-Hair's liquid eyes upon me and I rose to speak again. I felt surprisingly calm.

"I agree with Eye-of-the-Sun. If you open the tribes to the media, then you cannot control what happens in these lands. The technology and electricity that they promise will make life easier, will only bring misery and loneliness.

Our people promise things and then don't deliver. We lie and we cheat and we care only for profits. This is true. People will come here smiling with a snake in their hearts and they will look only for their own aggrandisement. Our tribe creates monopolies on food that mean that the nutritional factors are low, the land is destroyed and the animals suffer. Governments are corrupt, films are vacuous and tourists ignorant. Our people live in ivory towers of their own making and care nothing except to escape the fear and pain they won't face inside. Eye-of-the-Sun, I totally agree we cannot hear, see or feel. That is, most people cannot but a few can.

"There is a tide that is turning. In our tribe, there has always been those who are sensitive to the needs of others and share even in times of great suffering. There are those who tune into the rhythms of the earth and those who see a vision of the future, both of where we are heading and where we could go. There are those who abhor cruelty to animals and people. There are those who wish to feel and reach out to others.

"There is now a generation of people who feel lost and want to be found rocking in the embrace of Mother Earth. There are those who cry out in protest against the slaughter of whales and dolphins and the animals of the forest, rivers and deserts. There is a generation that does not want to inherit the 'sins of their fathers'. They have a vision of a different future. Our politics now have to address these issues or governments fall. It is, as yet, not a majority however it is growing all the time and the best way to touch these people and swell their numbers is through film. People also need to know what to do and how they can make change or they feel powerless and overwhelmed.

"If you do make a film, don't bring in people who may interpret it differently from what you want. Make something that you can distribute on the internet and create a groundswell of community support. Then you can interest the mainstream when you have already created a vision that is the way you want it. I think Jenny would be the perfect person to do this because you can trust her. She is of that new generation. She has felt the disconnection that our tribe feels deep inside and yet tries to hide, but Jenny doesn't want to hide. She has courage and is pure of heart. Even though she was brought up in the city, her heritage is here. She is the perfect bridge.

"On the internet, millions of people can see this film as a video and interact with their thoughts and feelings. You can outline the problems the way you see them. You can present the reality of what is happening, your fears and also a plan for hope. You can put forward what you want for the earth; people can also put forward what they feel they can do from their understanding of what is happening for them and what they see. It could be used like an online Gathering-of-the-Tribes but our tribes need not come here and you need not leave.

"I have to say the risk is as great as Eye-of-the-Sun says and you may not find it worth it. At the same time, as Wind-in-Her-Hair says, the destruction may become inevitable. Unless there is support gained from a wider community, there may be less hope for the future."

I sat down. It was strange to find myself talking so passionately when I really didn't have a solution and felt that both sides were right.

Bear-Heart then stood and spoke. I was surprised he did not attempt to influence the tribes one way or the other. He asked all the tribes to use their special skill and ability to access their intuition about the best course of action.

The tribes parted to meditate. They came back and discussed what they had heard, seen and felt. Instead of debating and putting down other's arguments, they incorporated the different points of view. They sought first to understand, and then saw if their plan could incorporate the insights of others. They ensured that solutions would offer safeguards and protection that incorporated everyone's concerns.

The scientists and anthropologists were pretty funny. Like me, they were not used to consensus decision-making. They would get all flustered or boosted up on the ego of their arguments, only to find the tribes asking questions and then incorporating their points of view into a cohesive whole. In the end, they relied on the unique intuition of each tribe to create an integrated solution.

I didn't participate much. I'd said all I could and didn't really have a side. To be honest, I probably sided most with Eye-of-the-Sun but that was more because I wanted the tribes all to myself. Of course, that had nothing to do with Eye-of-the-Sun's motivations which were, like his person, purely altruistic. If he was angry, it was on behalf of the tribes and the earth, and that seemed perfectly reasonable to me.

Instead, for me it was more like I'd found Aladdin's cave and didn't want anyone else to find the treasure. I know that sounds awfully selfish but since coming to these tribes, I realised just how incredibly self-centred I am. I hadn't really thought about it before. I was doing my best to be more sensitive and understanding but realised I just wasn't that evolved yet. It was better for me to be still, quiet, listen and absorb. I realised that even the youngest tribal member was light years ahead of me. It was pretty humbling. At first I could feel my ego bluster against it. At times I felt my ego sulking in a corner of my mind. But after many months, I found myself just accepting my level of growth and maturity and simply opening myself up to whatever I could do.

It was quite a relief to feel things weren't MY decision but rather OUR decision. I realised that all the control I felt I needed to protect my ego just was no longer necessary. I suppose that was because I felt loved and accepted – how simple that sounds. I wondered how our tribe could get it so wrong. I didn't mean it in some New Age hippy way but just on a very practical level. I had never realised just how foundational it was to belong and feel a sense of wellbeing and happiness. It was amazing how many things that I used to think were necessary no longer were. I no longer missed my video games, my phone or my computer – they just seemed irrelevant. Oh look, I get it – some of them are important tools – but that was it. I realised that I had been addicted to them. I was trying to use them to distract myself or to gain some form of connection, but they always left me feeling dissatisfied.So I wanted more and more trying to fill the empty hole inside. Now I don't feel like I have a hole. I just feel satisfied. I feel happy and content or upset and angry and it's all okay.

I could see Jenny blossoming under the acceptance of the tribe and their interest in her. As a result, her energy became more and more calm and she looked increasingly like Crystal-Call but with Wind-in-Her-Hair's warmth. At first I worried about my growing attraction to her. I wondered if it was just that she was beginning to remind me of Wind-in-Her-Hair, but I started to see beyond that and into her soul. I found myself falling in love with Jenny for herself; her enthusiasm, her passion and most of all her complete integrity.

One day, right in the middle of thinking about Jenny, Bear-Heart slapped me on the back almost winding me. It was his amused way of mocking our tribe's masculine bonding: "You're doing well, Surrogate Son." Then he patted me on the back in his normal way and nodded with a twinkle in his eye.

ACT 3, SCENE 16

JAVIER BEGINS TO OPEN HIS HEART TO HIS LITTLE SISTER

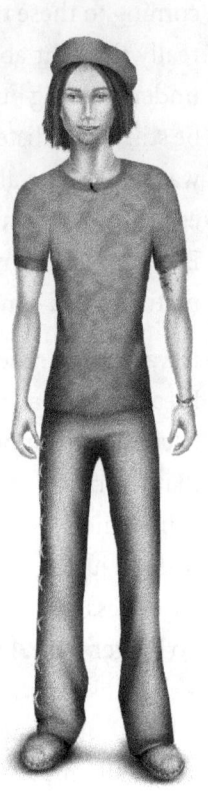

Okay, I totally get that I am being unreasonable but the thing going on between Andrew and Jenny was just freaking me out. Not that I thought anything had happened yet but all the looks and shy smiles and stuff – it was just plain nauseating. I don't know why his total obsession with Wind-in-Her-Hair didn't bother me at all. I suppose because Wind-in-Her-Hair could look after herself and Jenny was my little sister.

I pulled Andrew over one day and asked him what was going on and he just looked at me, smiled and said: "You know, Javier, this is one thing that is none of your business and I don't think that needs any translation, right?"

Then he just walked off. Who would have thought that Andrew would have the balls to speak to me like that! But the worst part about it was I knew he was right. I started to watch them like a panther stalking prey. At the same time a part of my mind stood cynically mocking me. After all, this was the most amount of attention I had ever given Jenny. Most of my life I had virtually ignored her and yet she was all the family I had. I found myself obsessing about them and I was so irrationally angry with Andrew. I could hear myself saying stuff in my head like:

"Who's he? He's been in the tribes about a minute and he already thinks he runs the place. He's like a son to Bear-Heart, a brother to Wind-in-Her-Hair and now he wants to claim Jenny. Well, I can't do anything about the first two but Jenny's mine, my family, and he can't have her."

I couldn't believe I was saying stuff like that, even to myself. What was I turning into, some kind of male chauvinist? Did I think I owned people? Did I think I was some kind of patriarch? After all, I'd left Jenny to look after herself. I had sent her off when she was little to aunts and uncles in the city, while I spent all my time with the tribes. Where was all my concern then? It didn't matter how I tried to spin it to myself, my anger had nothing to do with protecting Jenny. She was now an adult and perfectly capable of looking after herself. Besides that, where was the threat? Andrew was a decent guy. To be honest, it would be far better for Jenny to involve herself with someone like Andrew than someone like me.

So what sort of person did that make me? I had never really thought about it before. Somehow I had always felt, I don't know, some how special. I could speak all the languages. I was the only outsider truly accepted by all the tribes. I belonged everywhere and, well actually, nowhere. I was starting to wonder if I even liked myself very much. I'd always thought belonging nowhere was freedom. I don't know why I wanted that more than anything else. All of my relationships were casual. I didn't have relationships with women from the tribe because if I was involved, I would really need to think of marriage and I wasn't keen on the idea. One thing was certain, I never wanted to disrespect anyone in the three local tribes.

So I would have casual affairs with female scientists, anthropologists or the particularly adventurous female tourist. We didn't get the totally vacuous tourist here, not yet anyway, because they didn't know about these tribes. We weren't on any 'show and tell' tourist map. Eye-of-the-Sun saw to it that that never happened, since his tribal lands created a kind of buffer to everywhere else. He would be really hostile to anyone who just showed up. He'd let me take people around his land to Bear-Heart's tribe but that was about the only way anyone could get access.

So two or three times a year, a female outsider would find me through word of mouth and engage me as a translator or guide. I never made a move. They always did. I think they thought I looked like Che Guevara. They told me that often enough. Our conversations would go something like this:

Her: "You know you really look like Che Guevara."

I would think 'okay here we go' and I would say: "If you think so". Then she would say: "Don't you ever get lonely out here?"

That was really my cue. If I liked her I'd say: "Yeah, it can get pretty lonely." Even though I never felt that way. If I didn't like her, or just didn't feel like it, I'd say: "No, actually. I feel pretty content." And that was it. If I said the first, she would usually come and cuddle up to me and if I said the second, she would turn over and go to sleep.

But the weirdest thing was that now I see Jenny and Andrew spending time together, I think I'm jealous. I thought I'd never have that feeling, and if I was jealous then I couldn't be content with where I was, could I? There must be some connection that weedy Andrew was getting that I really wanted or why would I feel jealous? Then I would just feel furiously angry with Andrew. Before he came I felt fine. I wish he hadn't come and then I wouldn't feel this way. I wish he'd just leave, but if he was involved with Jenny, he might never be completely out of my life. Then I might feel like this forever! That would be really bad because I had a lurking suspicion that underneath all the anger, I was actually depressed.

I sat next to Bear-Heart the other day and he said to me: "You know, Javier, you're in your head a lot these days."

"No, I'm not. I'm feeling a lot of emotions; they are just not all that positive," I snapped back.

"Yep, in your head," he said with a smile: "A bear with a sore head." Then he laughed and wandered off. I was infuriated and was about to swear under my breath, when suddenly he was in front of me. For a big man, he could sure move quietly. Then he said: "Oh, by the way, it's good for you. Help you do something with that pride of yours." Then he wandered off again chuckling, before I could take a swipe at him.

ACT 3, SCENE 17

ANDREW AND JENNY FALL IN LOVE

I was falling head over heels in love with Jenny and we hadn't even kissed yet.

It was so different from the way I had fallen in love before. Previously, love had been an escape from the colourless world of drudgery my life had become. It was like a magical place where there was just me and the other person in some kind of bubble. That would be great for months and then the real world would intrude and burst the bubble. Like there would be assignments for uni due, or one of us would have to get a part-time job and we couldn't spend all of our time together. Then we would be fighting about the fact that we couldn't get our needs met and 'pop' – the bubble would burst – and it was "all over red rover." Sorry about the clichés but I do tend to think in them.

With Jenny it was different because I didn't need to escape from anything. I was blissfully happy and so was she and we could share our world together. Things didn't intrude, they were included. They were a part of the way we felt about each other.

The tribes finally agreed to let Jenny video them but their location was to remain a secret. We all decided to video everything in snippets and create an on-line TV show. Each segment was 5 minutes long. It was called *4 Tribes 1 Earth*. We would show pictures of the snow receding and the impact it was having on the forest and then people could write their comments and we would blog. Then the next segment would be someone from the tribes or a scientist answering a question. Then there were forums of what one could do about pollution and global warming and so on.

Sometimes the old cynical me would come back and I would wonder if it would ever make a difference. So on the website, Jenny set up a counter and people could put in that they had just reused a water bottle or created a worm farm. Then the online calculator would show how many tonnes of waste that would be saved if ten people did that every day and one hundred people and a thousand people. Scientists would log on and calculate how much electricity that would save and therefore fossil fuel consumption. Then people would pledge their commitment. Last I saw we had just hit the ten thousand mark of new people with worm farms. It was pretty exciting. The guy who sold the worm farms had a policy of giving free worm farms to tea growers in India. He was ecstatic. He was able to help so many poor farmers increase their yields of tea by using fertilises made from organic waste eaten by worms. They were in the process of getting organic certification and this would give them an extra point of difference. We also advertised their tea on the site and they had a huge increase in sales. That was pretty exciting. Even if we couldn't stop global warming, we had helped those people and their children. That had to be worth something no matter what.

Then all the people with worm farms started getting interested in their gardens because they had to pour the worm juice somewhere. Some people didn't plant anything and they would find pumpkins just self-seeding. One girl was so excited. She hadn't been home for a little while and then she was showing some visitors around her tiny city garden and just sitting there was a fully grown pumpkin on the vine. She said it was magical. She picked up the pumpkin, took it inside and made pumpkin soup. Her visitors were so impressed that they decided to get a worm farm too. There were also people putting excess worm juice on their nature strip and finding trees started to flower twice a year instead of once a year, so then more bees and birds came.

Jenny and I were over the moon. That was the first day we kissed. We were jumping up and down when we saw the worm farm sales hit ten thousand and threw our arms about each other. Then we pulled back and looked into each other's eyes. I then cupped her face in my hands and very slowly and deliberately placed a tender kiss on each cheek like Wind-in-Her-Hair had done for me in friendship.

Jenny giggled and said, "I think we might be more than friends" and she grabbed the back of my neck and drew me to her and kissed me right on the lips with complete abandon. It was so funny, so unlike the other tribes, we just both burst out laughing like two naughty school kids. That was the great thing about Jenny and me – we could just be ourselves. We could draw in what we had learnt from the other tribes to enhance our own beings and then – I don't know quite how to put it – just be.

We had been travelling back and forth from the tribes to the city so we could set up the website and at the same time keep the tribes informed of our progress. We would video them answering people's questions and give them feedback from the site. They would also take the camera and just film themselves and we would receive back the most amazing footage. Sometimes it would be weeks before we would get the camera back and there would be hours of footage of a waterfall and all the animals that visited it. It took me a while to realise that the footage wasn't about the visuals but about the sounds. Of all people, Crystal-Call had taken the camera to Echo Canyon and recorded the sounds with the waterfall as a backdrop. Well, that's how she experienced it. Then there was the sound of the tribe harmonising the music of nature into a song. It was so exquisitely beautiful that I cried. I had never heard anything like it.

She then said to me with a smile: "Can you put this on the website and then ask for donations so we can have a camera for each of the tribes?" I was sure that we could. Within a month we had enough money for the cameras and we had all these calls for a recording contract. It was pretty funny. I told Crystal-Call that they wanted to make her a singing sensation and for the first time I heard her really, really laugh like carillon bells chiming.

Wind-in-Her-Hair had catalogued a hundred seeds from the forest and their medicinal use. We decided it was enough to approach the Central Seed Library. They accepted the seeds and were growing and testing them. We knew we had to step carefully about their benefits. No one was naïve about the monopoly, power or danger of drug companies. "Softly, slowly steps the big cat that is the most successful," said Wind-in-Her-Hair once when I was feeling particularly frustrated.

So things were happening and there seemed to be hope, however as much as we did our best to water, the forest kept dying. It really, really needed rain. We prayed, we worked and we planned every day. Bear-Heart allowed a wooden channel made from dead trees to direct water to the forest but only once a week. He said any more than that and the other tribes would suffer.

"There are things I know," Bear-Heart said to me, "which go beyond what short-sighted science knows. There are consequences for every action in nature and if we interfere too much, somewhere else an imbalance is created. We must continue to work at redressing the imbalance in your tribe's way of life, rather than interfering too much here. In the long term, it is best. I know it in my soul, even if my heart breaks with each dying tree."

So that is where we are up to. We have created an invisible bridge between our two worlds that allows for communication without exploitation. I only hope that soon, before it's too late, storm clouds will gather over the Forest of Rain and rather than unleashing destruction, they will "Droppeth as the gentle rain from heaven upon the place beneath."

EPILOGUE

JENNY SPEAKS ABOUT THEIR SHARED DREAM

So Wind-in-Her-Hair and Bright-Eagle were able to have their wedding during the Gathering-of-the-Tribes without it turning into a media event. They would have sacrificed their privacy, if it had meant making a difference to the forest and the earth as a whole, but it wasn't necessary.

The website was a way that Bear-Heart could open up communication between the tribes without having to sacrifice privacy. So that worked out well and everyone was really happy. He's a wise man to see that the combined thinking of all the tribes would be able to come up with a better solution than he could on his own, especially when our tribe was the problem.

Andrew and I are still together. We have decided to take things slowly and build our relationship on a solid foundation.

The *4 Tribes 1 Earth Movement* grows every day and has a life of its own as people have more and more ideas that they share and build communities of support. It operates on a similar principle as the Gathering-of-the-Tribes except it's on the web. Even if in the end we cannot save the forest or even the earth, the Movement is worthwhile for the joy and hope that it brings. I still believe we will have critical mass and make a shift before it's too late. Andrew, I know, is not so sure but he believes that we must do everything we can.

We don't personally take any money from donations but put all that money straight into projects. One seven-year-old girl donates five cents from her pocket money every week and we find her such an inspiration. We draw an income and running expenses from the selected ads we run for services that are truly sustainable and social enterprises. That gives us the funds we need to travel the world and live while we go to various conferences and give speeches. Someone donated a house to us which doubles as our headquarters and home, which is very cool, and it's often full of visiting community members.

In the end, we had to build a garden room in the backyard, all from recycled materials of course, just so Andrew and I could get away from it all. We needed to and give our relationship some special time. We want our lives to have meaning within and outside our growing love. So we spend time alone and have our own set of friends and interests as well as those we share. That wasn't easy to do because we are both so passionate about *4 Tribes 1 Earth*. We know that it's easy to burn out if you don't find some balance. Being out of balance is the whole problem with modern society and the earth – so we didn't want a cure to turn out to be another part of the problem.

Bear-Heart has been a great mentor in keeping us grounded and of course our dear friend, Wind-in-Her-Hair. She is pretty much Chieftess of the Tribe-that-Moves-and-is-Touched now. Bear-Heart spends more and more time meditating; he says he wants to spend time in union with the heart of the earth. I'm not exactly sure what that means but it seems very important to him. No doubt it serves a purpose that no one can see but the earth feels.

Javier came and spoke to me one day. He apologised for the way he had treated me when we were growing up. That really took me by surprise – I had never really thought about it. He was always my big brother and I worshipped the ground he walked on, so everything he did seemed warranted to me. So I was even more surprised by my reaction. I suddenly felt really, really angry with him. I thought: *Yeah, actually you abandoned me when I needed you the most.* Generally his presence made me feel like I was somehow not good enough to warrant his attention. It seemed like I was constantly annoying him.

So that's what I told him. He said:

"I am happy you're angry, Jenny, because that means you believe that you deserve to be treated better, and that is true."

I thought that was kind of ironic that my anger was a symbol of my growing self-esteem. Before I had just been happy for whatever scraps of attention he was willing to throw my way and that had been the pattern of pretty much all of my relationships. Now I know I deserve better than that. I feel like I actually warrant respect and attention. It helps that I feel part of something important and more than anything else, I truly belong. I have found my tribe.

Why couldn't he have just given me that? Why did he have to withdraw in the face of my desperate pain? Why couldn't he have held me and given me the attention I wanted?

But then I realised that my raw pain reminded him of his hidden pain and he just couldn't face it. I felt sad for him. In many ways he was still alone. He just couldn't be vulnerable enough to reach out. I don't really understand why. Sometimes I felt like saying to him: "Come out of your ivory tower. It's no different for you than for anyone else. We all go through it." Sometimes I feel really judgemental and think he's just weak. So you can see I was still angry within and it was eating me up. So when he said he was going on a retreat to the Vision Caves in the Painted Desert, I was truly furious.

"You're lonely so you want to solve your problem by being alone," I shouted at him, which was probably inappropriate. He just looked at me and gave me one of those enigmatic smiles which infuriated me even more.

Wind-in-Her-Hair, who happened to be there, put her hand on my arm and said: "We all deal with our pain in different ways. Yours is to reach out. Javier's is to withdraw."

I shrugged her off: "With all due respect, Wind-in-Her-Hair, you haven't been on the receiving end of this your whole life. You haven't had the only person you love left in the world rejecting and abandoning you. So don't go about excusing him."

"You're right, Jenny. It's not something that happens in my tribe. I don't know how you feel. What I do know is that if Javier had behaved differently, you may not have gone off and found the tools that we are finding so useful now. Is that really selfish of me?"

Wind-in-Her-Hair selfish? – that would be the day – however I still felt upset. Intellectually I knew she was right, of course, but I didn't care. I could still remember night after night feeling alone, sad and scared, and crying and crying until my stomach hurt and I ran out of breath.

Javier could feel how distressed I was and tried to put his arms around me saying, "I'm so sorry. I love you, Jenny I really do." But I couldn't handle it and pushed him away and walked off.

In the end, it was Andrew who helped me heal. I bet Javier would have found that ironic considering his disdain for the Tribe-that-Thinks-and-Calculates. Andrew had been changed, howevere by his time in the Dying Forest and he too could feel and be sensitive.

I decided I wanted to go to the Vision Caves before Javier started his retreat there. I'm not sure why. Perhaps I wanted to see what was so important that he was going to sacrifice his newfound connection with me. So Andrew and I garnered permission from Eye-of-the-Sun and set out. By the end of the day we found the cliff's raw edges and climbed up into the caves.

The paintings were so exquisitely beautiful that I felt instantly mesmerised by the play of colour. The paintings seemed to dance in the dappled light from the opening.

After what seemed like an age, Andrew said:

"When I asked permission for us to come to these caves, Eye-of-the-Sun gave me a message for you. He said: 'Tell Jenny that the pictures on the walls speak about a vision of the future as well as frame the pictures of the past. It is Javier's role to see that vision and translate it into a language that paints a picture in the minds of others. The problem is that Javier has been a translator for so long that he has become lost between the tribes instead of belonging to the tribes. He looks lonely because he has forgotten how to see his own soul's vision. He needs to go to the caves so he can see inside' himself to reconnect."

Then Andrew took my hand and said:

"When my mother died, I blamed my father; his coldness and his lack of communication allowed me to project all my unhealed pain onto him. In the end my mother would have died even if my father had been a different man. It was her time to die, like this is our time to live".

Then we were quiet with tears rolling down our faces while we stared at the paintings on the walls. The ancient pictures blurred and reformed into a vision that whispered to us of a new future. Our hearts opened up to the possibility of four tribes and one earth living in harmony.

The End

SECTION 2

The Different Tribes

UNDERSTANDING EACH TRIBE
AND HOW TO USE
COMMUNICATION STYLES

In Business, Teaching, Coaching
and Personal Development
as told by the characters

> Want to experience a quiz to find out which
> Communication Tribe you belong to? Then go to
> 4 Tribes 1 Earth Quiz at www.pipmckay.com.au/4tribes1earth
> and come back here to read more.

YOUR SCORE

Although your highest score may be in one tribe, you may also have points in another tribe and this will also affect the way you communicate and learn. As a result, to understand yourself and others more deeply, it is important to study all of the tribes and their characteristics.

The two tribes that are your lowest score are worth considering too because these tribes have a very different way of interacting than you do. So this is the place where you have the most to learn. Often the people we think are difficult will be from the tribes that have our lowest score in the quiz. If you learn about those tribes, then you will find it is easier to get on with a wider range of people. This can be very useful in your career, particularly if you deal with different types of people, and it may also solve many problems in your relationships.

As you read Section 2 we assume you have already read Section 1 but this section will make sense on its own.

GENERAL INTRODUCTION TO THE TRIBES

Once upon a time there were four tribes:

1. The Tribe-that-Sees-and-has-Visions
2. The Tribe-that-Moves-and-is-Touched
3. The Tribe-that-Listens-and-Sings
4. The Tribe-that-Thinks-and-Calculates

The tribes grew up separately in isolated areas of the earth. They developed their own unique culture based on the **SENSE** they most favoured. This created their unique way of communicating.

In our modern world, the four tribes have combined, yet each person still uses a dominant sense and this affects their personality, likes and behaviour. It also influences the way they communicate and learn.

When you find out your communication tribe, you feel a tremendous sense of belonging. You more deeply understand yourself and your interaction with others. It also gives you a clear direction for personal development, making it easier to fulfill your potential by embracing your genius and enhancing areas that are less strong.

When you understand another's tribe you get on with more people more easily. There is less conflict and greater peace and harmony.

Each communication tribe is just a habit of learning and processing information. We can change and adapt our preferences with practice and enhance our experience of the world.

In the corporate environment, teams become easier to manage and lead and are more cooperative when they understand different modes of communication. Productivity goes up and absenteeism goes go down because everyone is much happier in a supportive corporate culture.

In relationships, it becomes easier to maintain acceptance, understanding and love because you get where the other person is coming from.

In schools, it makes it easier for all children to be motivated, learn and reach their potential because the information is presented in a way that they can comprehend. In the following pages each tribe is described in detail. You will learn:

1. Each tribe's gifts and talents
2. How to recognise each tribe
3. How to communicate and build rapport with each tribe
4. How each tribe learns and therefore how to teach them effectively
5. What each tribe is like in relationships – their needs and desires
6. Different types of tribal members within each tribe
7. How to develop the sense and gifts of each tribe to accelerate your personal development and growth
8. About your scores

TRIBE-THAT-SEES-AND-HAS-VISIONS
Narrated by Bright-Star and Bright-Eagle

General Introduction

As the name of our tribe suggests, we like to observe and imagine. We favour visual information which means we take most notice of what we see. As a result, we are often visually artistic and interested in design or ensuring things look beautiful, or at least neat and tidy. We tend to be well dressed and well groomed. People like us because we are observant, bring clarity to projects, information or environments and can see the big picture. Sometimes when people are messy or unkempt we find this very distracting but generally we understand that people don't always see things the way we do.

1. How To Recognise Us

We tend to sit upright so we can see everything, breathe high in our chest and speak quickly with a high tone of voice. We like clothing that is beautiful or makes us look good. We tend to be tidy and organized because we like things to look neat. We use words such as 'see', 'look' and 'imagine'. We have catchphrases like: "Let me see" or "Picture this!"

Apparently we make up about 40% of the city population but through the quiz, Andrew and Jenny (our resident researchers) will be able to collect more accurate data.

2. How To Communicate and Build Rapport With Us

If you want us to see you as part of our tribe and trust you, then it is important that you:

- Sit up straight and breathe high in the chest (no slouching or we will secretly see you as lazy)
- Speak quickly with a higher tone of voice (or we will secretly see you as slow and boring)
- Make an effort with your appearance and tidiness (or we will secretly see you as unkempt and uncouth)
- Draw pictures when explaining something complicated – then we can see what you mean
- Paint a picture with words and use words like 'imagine', 'picture', 'see' and 'look'.

If you show us these qualities then in return, we are more likely to see things from your point of view as well as understand and accept what you say.

3. How To Teach Us So We Learn Effectively From You

We learn best by seeing diagrams and pictures and we like teachers who show us how to do something or use visual aids. If we can picture something then we can learn very quickly. If we can't get an image of verbal instructions then we can't. We are easily distracted by bright colours, anything that's mismatching or a mess. In our tribe everything is taught through drawings in the sand or on the cave walls or through stories that paint a picture with words.

4. What We Are Like In Relationships

In relationships we like to gaze into our partner's eyes. For us, the eyes are definitely the windows to the soul. One of the ways we show people we like them is to dress well for them and we like it when they notice. We also show appreciation of the way others look by taking notice of changes they make in the way they do their hair and how they dress. We imagine that someone is being disrespectful when they don't make an effort to make themselves or their environment visually pleasing.

We are not particularly affectionate in public as we do not think that looks very good to other members of the tribe. It is important to us how we appear to the world and we display social status by how our partner and we look. Some other tribes are judgemental of this and think that we are shallow but because we take so much notice of what we see, this just seems normal to us. It doesn't necessarily have to be beauty that we are looking for, although we do appreciate that, but it is more that someone shows they are respectful of themselves and others by taking care of their appearance.

5. Different Types of Members of Our Tribe

Our tribe is divided into two types, 'Seers' and 'Imaginers', and some people are both.

Seers are very observant. They notice what you wear and changes in the way you look and they like visual order, fashion and design. People sometimes comment that they are critical, perfectionistic and superficial, but this heightened observation can make them visually gifted.

Imaginers see visions in their mind's eye and like to create visual images including visual arts, film and photography. People sometimes comment that they are daydreamers but this heightened ability to visualise can make them highly artistic.

6. How to Enhance Your Sense of Sight and Develop Visual Talents

Make a vow to spend a day totally focused on what you see: colour, shape, texture and changes in what you see. Do the following exercises to help you:

Visual Exercise 1 – Practicing Visual Recall

Close your eyes and visualise the colour red. Open your eyes and take notice of everything in the room that is red. Close your eyes and recall all the things that are red in the room. Open your eyes and see if you remembered everything. Close your eyes and repeat until you can visually recall everything that is red. Then repeat the process with everything that is green, blue, yellow, brown etc.

Visual Exercise 2 – Practicing Imagination

This is a great exercise if you don't find it easy to visualise or imagine. It uses your other senses to lead you in.

Think of lying on the beach on your back on a towel. Get a feeling of the warmth of the sand under your body, the texture of the towel, the warmth of the sun above you and the feeling of your bathers. They are wet and you can feel them cold and wet compared to the warmth of the towel on the sand.

Now you can hear some seagulls squawking, some children laughing and squealing, some people talking and the gentle crash of the waves on the sand. You open your eyes and look at the blue sky. You see a seagull flying above you. You sit up and look at the ocean. You can see a yacht with a white sail. There is a child with its father going into the ocean, the child has red bathers on and the father has blue Hawaiian boardshorts. Is the child a boy or a girl? Do they have a hat on? What colour is the hat?

Congratulations. You have just been visualising!

Visual Exercise 3 – Using Visual Cues to Enhance Intuition About People

Watch someone closely who is talking with you, who you know well. Take notice of their changes of expression, changes of colour in their face, pupil dilation, lower lip size and colour, as well as the pattern of their eye movements when they are thinking.

When you see changes in any of these things, or anything else, see if you can guess what it means. Is the person feeling a particular emotion? Do they like what they are talking about, dislike it or feel embarrassed or emotional? Are they imagining something? Can you imagine what they are imagining? Guess, and then if it is appropriate, respectfully ask them for verification. It is usually best to just ask: "What do you feel about that?" or "What are you picturing in your head right now?"

When someone looks up they are accessing visual information – either visual memory or imagination. When you see their eyes go up then this is a good time to ask them what they are picturing in their mind.

TRIBE-THAT-MOVES-AND-IS-TOUCHED

Narrated by Wind-in-Her-Hair and Bear-Heart

General Introduction

As the name of our tribe suggests, we like to move physically and/or be touched emotionally. Some of our tribe like both of these things but often members of our tribe are either 'Doers' or 'Feelers'. Our favoured sense is kinesthetic which means "to move." We tend to be good at sport, building things, massage or emotional healing and counselling depending on our type. People like us because we are either physically coordinated or empathetic and understanding. Sometimes we find that people can be uncaring and insensitive in return and we can find this hurtful or we may feel impatient if people are impractical or uncoordinated but generally we are understanding and do our best to make people feel good.

1. How To Recognise Us

We tend to sit back and be relaxed, breathe into our stomach and speak slowly and deeply. If you think Angelina Jolie, the werewolf from the *Twilight* movie (Jacob Black) or sports stars, then you get the feeling. However, unlike our Hollywood counterparts, we tend to like clothing that is comfortable or makes us feel good. We are sometimes a bit disorganised and messy, but we make up for that by generally being good with people. We like to use words such as 'do', 'feel' and 'grasp'. We have catchphrases like: "Let's do something!" or "I know how you feel."

Apparently we make up about 40% of the city population but through the quiz, Andrew and Jenny (our resident researchers) will be able to collect more accurate data.

2. How To Communicate and Build Rapport With Us

If you want us to feel comfortable with you and trust you, then it is important that you:

- Sit back, relax and breathe into your stomach (no sitting upright or we will secretly feel like you're uptight and tense)
- Speak slowly with a low tone of voice (or we will secretly feel that you are speedy and shallow)
- Be comfortable in your clothing and home (or we will secretly feel uncomfortable and judged in your presence)
- Do an activity or give an example in the real world when you're explaining something, so we can grasp what you mean
- Get in touch with feelings or actions when talking by using words like 'feel', 'do', 'grasp', 'touch' and 'take action'.

If you do this then we will feel comfortable with you and be in touch with your feelings and actions as well. Then we are more likely to understand and accept what you say.

3. How To Teach Us So We Learn Effectively From You

We learn best by doing activities and we like teachers who know how we feel, create exercises and use models. Sometimes we don't find it easy to follow verbal instructions or things in sequential order. But if you take us through how to do something physically, we will usually remember it. We have great body memory and are often good at sports, performance and connecting with others.

We are generally very in touch with our feelings, so if we are angry or upset, or sense that you are angry or upset that makes it not easy for us to concentrate. If you want to teach us effectively, it is important that you are honest with your feelings (because we can sense them anyway) or that you are in a good state emotionally when teaching us, otherwise we will find your emotions distracting. Sometimes other people's emotions are so overwhelming for us that we act out or are disruptive but this is just because in modern culture there is not much outlet for emotions. We can also have a lot of excess energy that builds up when we have to sit still for long periods of time.

In our tribe we learn by doing, from storytelling where we can emotionally connect with the characters, or by being in touch with a teacher we like. If this happens we find it quick and easy to learn. If it doesn't, then we can get a bit lost in the learning environment.

4. What We Are Like In Relationships

In relationships, we are affectionate and passionate. We do not like people who are cold, in their heads or too caught up with how they look. How our partner feels is very important to us and we will go to great lengths to make them happy. We feel loved and loving by holding hands publicly, touching and demonstrating affection. Some other tribes may think that we are clingy but we just like feeling connected to those we love.

We like to do activities with our partner as well as have quiet nights at home cuddling up. We can generally talk about emotions but if we are emotionally overwhelmed, we may clam up and shut off because we don't know what to do. Beauty to us is how someone feels when we hold them in our arms, how they make us feel and who they are on the inside. Love and passion are core to our very being.

5. Different Types of Members of Our Tribe

Our tribe is divided into two types, 'Doers' and 'Feelers', and some people are both.

Doers are very physical. They like sport, movement and working with their hands. They are often told that they never sit still, but this hyperactivity leads to being gifted in physical activity.

Feelers are very in touch with their own and other people's emotions. People like to go to them to be understood, counselled or nurtured. They are often told that they are too sensitive but this quality often leads them to be gifted in human interactions.

6. How to Enhance Your Sense of Touch and Develop Emotional Talents

Make a vow to spend a day totally focused on what you feel both physically and emotionally. Do the following exercises to help you.

Kinesthetic Exercise 1 – Feeling and Creating Emotional Intelligence

Close your eyes and get in touch with your body, particularly your solar plexus (above your belly button and below your ribs), your belly and your heart. What are the physical sensations in those parts of your body? Does it feel constricted and uncomfortable or free and comfortable? What shape is the feeling? Does the sensation move or is it still? Does it have a temperature or a weight? What emotional word would you put to that sensation?

Does that sensation give you the emotional message of sadness, anger, happiness or excitement? What is causing this emotion? Did someone say something to you? Are things going well or not well for you in your life? When did you start feeling this way? What happened then? If you feel uncomfortable, what can you do to make yourself feel better? Is there a friend or someone close to you who you can talk to about this feeling? What happens to this feeling when you talk about it?

Kinesthetic Exercise 2 – Getting In Touch With Sensations and Feelings

This is a great exercise if you don't find it easy to know how you are feeling. It uses your other senses to lead you in.

Imagine looking at the beach. See the yellow sand and the blue water. Really see the different colours of the water – turquoise, dark blue – and then the bright blue of the sky above it. Look at the children playing on the beach. One little boy has red Hawaiian boardshorts on and another little girl is wearing a pink hat. The children are chasing seagulls around.

You can hear the seagulls squawking and the children laughing and squealing. You can also hear some people talking closer to you and the gentle crash of the waves in the background.

You are sitting on a towel and you can feel the warm sand underneath you and the sun on your back. The towel feels rough on the back of your calves and you can feel the gritty sand between your fingers. You feel a warm, round, comfortable feeling in your solar plexus and you realise that you feel relaxed and content.

Congratulations you have just been recognising feelings!

Kinesthetic Exercise 3 – Touching Others and Developing Empathy

Identify how you are feeling just in yourself without anyone else around. Get a sense of what is going on for you emotionally.

Then meet someone and sit with them while you chat. Ask them questions and get them to talk about what is happening for them, what is going on in their day, their family, relationship or work. Sit the same way they are sitting. If they are sitting forward then sit forward too. If they are sitting back and relaxed, sit that way too. If they have their hands on a table or in their lap, do the same. If they are using their hands to talk, keep your hands still unless it is your time to talk and then use similar gestures. Do this in a subtle respectful manner. This is called matching and mirroring body language and is a great way to get into rapport with people so that they feel comfortable around you.

Now become aware of your gut or solar plexus. Notice if you feel differently inside than you did when you were just by yourself. Do the feelings change depending on what the person is saying? Can you name those emotions? If they mention emotions, see if you can also feel those emotions inside yourself. Can you discern what are your emotional responses and what are theirs? If they haven't mentioned emotions and it is appropriate, then gently ask them what they are feeling and check inside yourself if that is the same as what you have guessed.

People usually access emotions when they look down so this might be a good time to ask. Be aware that people also look down when they are thinking, however if you ask, you will soon know if they are responding to questions about feeling or thinking.

Remember people often feel vulnerable about their emotions so take your time, gain trust and be sensitive in your approach. In the end, creating the space for people to talk about their feelings is one of the greatest gifts you can give them.

They often feel less alone and happier after sharing, so long as they feel that they can trust you and you are open about discussing your emotions too. This is one of the most profound gifts of the Tribe-that-Moves-and-is-Touched and is why the other tribes seek them out. Even though we have a dominant tribe, we can still benefit from the gifts of tribes that are different from our own.

TRIBE-THAT-LISTENS-AND-SINGS
Narrated by Bird-Song and Whispering-Spirit

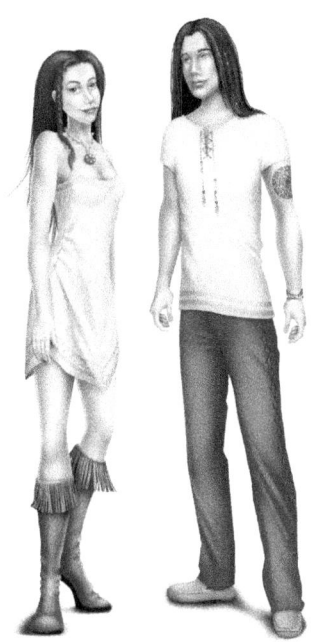

General Introduction

As the name of our tribe suggests, we like to spend time listening. We favour auditory information which means we take most notice of what you hear. As a result, we are often musical or at least love listening to music. We do like to talk too and discuss information but only if someone really wants to listen. We tend to have beautiful voices and can easily replay sounds, accents or conversations. People like us because we listen carefully, remember what they say and can follow verbal instructions. Sometimes we find that people do not listen to us in return and we consider that disrespectful but we do understand that not everyone likes to listen in the way we do.

1. How To Recognise Us In Your World

We often sit or stand with our head on the side so that we can listen more intently. Whereas other tribes are either laid back or very upright, instead we sit somewhere in the middle. We breathe into our mid chest and speak at a medium pace with a variety of tone and rhythm. People often say our voices are enjoyable to listen to. We like music, singing and the sounds of nature. We find it easy to think in a sequential order and remember verbal information. We like to use words such as 'listen', 'hear' and 'tone'. We have catchphrases like: "Sounds good to me!" or "You're not listening to me."

Apparently we make up about 10% of the city population, which makes us one of the smallest tribes. Through the quiz, Andrew and Jenny (our resident researchers) will be able to collect more accurate data.

2. How To Communicate And Build Rapport With Us

If you want to be in harmony with our tribe and for us to trust you, then it is important that you:

- Often have your head on one side and remember what we say (otherwise we get a sense that you don't listen and we think that is disrespectful)
- Sit somewhere between relaxed and upright and breathe into the mid chest (or we secretly think you are too upright or too laid back)
- Speak beautifully with a variety of tone and pace (or you sound unharmonious to us and we can secretly find that hard to listen to)
- We are more interested in how you sound then how you look, so paying attention to that is important to us
- We love to listen and be listened to, but because we are such good listeners, we rarely find people outside our own tribe who are as skilled in this way. So make sure you ask us questions and really listen to our answers, and then ask more questions that show you heard
- You may like to ask us to repeat certain things back by saying: "I just want to make sure I was really listening and understood. So you said . . ." Then repeat what we say word for word. That will make us very happy
- We love music and musical words so if you can make any reference to these we will be impressed

If you speak and listen to us with these qualities, then we will listen, understand and accept what you say more easily.

3. How To Teach Us So We Learn Effectively From You

We learn best by listening to information or repeating what is said inside our mind or out loud. We remember verbal instructions, lectures and utterances in the order and sequence in which they are told. We are sensitive to tone of voice and do not like it when people raise their voices or are verbally harsh. If you speak to us like that then we tend to tune out and will not learn easily. We love it when a teacher asks questions and opens up interesting topics of discussion. We are good at learning languages, can read well and tend to do well at studies. Sometimes it is not so easy for us to see the big picture, as we tend to be occupied with the details, order and sequence of information.

We love to learn by listening to stories, poetry or word games. We like mnemonic prompts, rhyming couplets and playing with how tone changes the meaning of utterances. We love to learn music and may remember information by creating a song.

4. What We Are Like In Relationships

In relationships, we like to listen intently to others and love it when they return the favour. There is nothing like a good discussion, listening to good music or the sounds of nature together. We really like words and have a good vocabulary. Our biggest problem in relationships with people outside our tribe is that, because we are such good listeners and others love to talk, we may feel like no-one is listening to us or is taking the time to ask questions and listen to the answers. We also like the sound of silence and really know we love someone when we can sit comfortably in silence and hear each other's thoughts.

5. Different Types of Members of Our Tribe

Our tribe is divided into two types, 'Listeners' and 'Musicians' and some people are both.

As stated above, **Listeners** spend much of their time listening to other people however they often feel that no-one really hears them. They understand and remember what people are saying and are able to pick up variations in tone and accurately understand what that means. They also remember very clearly what someone has said, often word-for-word and in the right sequence and order. Because they spend so much time listening they can appear quiet and introverted. However when someone really listens to them and they feel safe, they open up and have a lot to say.

Musicians, as the name suggests, are amazing at creating music either with an instrument or as a singer. They remember lyrics easily and can play music by ear. They can easily replicate others and can be good mimics if they want to be. They may also create music inside their minds and then play it easily. They will have beautiful voices and spend much time ensuring they are pitch-perfect.

Be aware that just because you like music and singing doesn't mean you are necessarily a part of our tribe. You might like these things because of how they make you feel, rather than the actual sound. Most people have our tribe as part of their lowest score because we are a smaller tribe. So it's worthwhile getting to know us because when you explore your auditory senses in more depth, you will find a whole new world opens up to you.

6. How to Enhance Your Sense of Hearing and Develop Auditory Talents

Make a vow to spend a day totally focused on what you hear: tone of voice, rhythm, music and quality of sound. Do the following exercises to help you.

Auditory Exercise 1 – Being In Tune with Your World, Body and Intuition

Close your eyes and listen to the sounds in the room. Maybe there are computer, air conditioning or refrigerator sounds. Now listen to the sound just outside the room maybe there are bird sounds, car noises or wind. Now imagine that you can hear what is in the building next door. Who is talking? What are they saying? What is the tone and volume of their voice? Now tune into the sounds of your suburb. What does your suburb sound like? What does your city sound like? What does your country sound like? Zoom into different areas of your country such as the forest or desert. What are the sounds there? How are they different from each other? Now what does the whole world sound like? What does the solar systems sound like? Finally can you hear the sounds of the universe?

Now come back to what the solar system sounds like, the world, your country, your city, your suburb, your street and then inside your room. Now what are the sounds of your body? Can you hear your heartbeat? Scan your body. Are there parts of your body that are telling you they are uncomfortable, want to move, want to stretch? Is your body telling you that you are thirsty, hungry or satisfied? Are you tired, relaxed or happy? Listen to your emotions. Do they want to tell you anything? What about your intuition? Is there a question you want to ask your intuition? What does it say in response?

Auditory Exercise 2 – Getting In Tune With Sound

This is a great exercise if you don't find it easy to listen or imagine sound. It uses your other senses to lead you in.

Think of lying on the beach on your back on a towel. Get a feeling of the warmth of the sand under your body, the texture of the towel, the warmth of the sun above you and the feeling of your bathers. They are wet and you can feel them cold compared to the warmth of the towel on the sand.

Now imagine that you have opened your eyes and are looking at the blue sky. You see a seagull flying above you. You sit up and look at the ocean. You can see a yacht with a white sail. There is a little girl with her father going into the ocean. The girl is in pink bathers and the father has blue Hawaiian boardshorts.

Now you can hear the child squealing as a wave comes and wets her feet. The father is laughing. You can hear other children laughing as they run at some seagulls. The seagulls are squawking as they fly away. You can hear the swoop of wings as one seagull flies very close to you.

Congratulations! You have just been getting in tune with sound!

Auditory Exercise 3 – Using Auditory Cues to Enhance Intuition About People

Listen to someone closely who is talking with you, who you know well and ask questions that get them to continue talking. Listen for changes of tone, volume, speed and quality of their voice. When you hear these changes, ask yourself if you can guess what they mean. Is the change in their voice reflecting a different emotion, attitude or way of thinking? Are the words they are saying congruent with their tone of voice? For example, they may say that they are happy but their tone of voice may sound unenthusiastic or bored. When you hear these discrepancies gently ask them for verification. For example: "Are you sure you are feeling happy? It's just that you don't sound very happy. What is really going on for you?" Remember to watch your tone of voice when you ask questions like this. You might like to preframe this with: "Is it okay if I ask . . .

When someone's eyes go to one side or the other, they are accessing auditory information, either a memory or creating sounds in their head like music or a tune, or simply planning what they are going to say. When you see their eyes do this, then you might like to ask them what they can hear.

TRIBE-THAT-THINKS-AND-CALCULATES
Narrated by Jenny and Andrew

General Introduction
As the name of our tribe suggests, we spend a lot of time in our heads thinking about theories or calculations. The sense we favour is called Audio-Digital. It's not really a sense but rather a way of processing information by talking to ourselves or through digital or abstract thinking. As a result, we are often great at IT, mathematics, science or logic. People like us because we tend to be really smart, good at budgeting and great at technology. Sometimes we find that our interpersonal skills aren't so good and people say we don't care enough about their feelings but that doesn't make a lot of sense to us as we are generally polite.

1. How To Recognise Us
We tend to sit upright or crouched over a computer and breathe into our mid-chest and speak in a bit of a monotone. Think of Bill Gates or the guy who created Facebook, Mark Zuckerberg, and you have us in a nutshell. We don't tend to care much about how we dress but are more interested in thoughts, gadgets and factual details. We like lists and store steps in a flow chart, to-do lists or simply in our heads. It's easy for us to see all the steps that need to be taken to get an outcome or to think in systems or patterns. We can be quite obsessive when we have an idea or are creating a system and have a tendency to sit at a computer all day and night when needed. We like to use words such as 'think', 'idea', 'calculate', 'system' and 'concept'. We have catchphrases such as: "I think so" or "Interesting idea".

We make up only about 10% of the population but these statistics are old and we look forward to gathering more accurate data from our quiz. People sometimes think that we are difficult but we are not being so deliberately. We just tend to think differently from the other tribes. If you take the time to think about things from our point of view, however, you will find a whole new world opens up for your thinking pleasure. It's a good idea not to dismiss us because you can't understand us. Some of the greatest inventors and thinkers come from our tribe and we are usually at the forefront of new technology and ways of thinking.

We are also a growing tribe. As people use technology at younger ages, they move more into their heads. This can mean they begin to ignore how they feel and focus on thinking instead.

2. How To Communicate And Build Rapport With Us

If you want our tribe to take you seriously and trust you, then it is important that you:

- Are not too animated in your speech or movements (or we tend to think you're a bit over the top)
- Keep your voice monotonal and keep your information factual (nothing annoys us more than inaccurate information or a lack of research)
- We are not interested in how you feel or what you look like. We are interested in how you think. Keep it logical not emotional (or we think that you're flaky and not in control)
- Discuss interesting ideas, gadgets, facts and features
- Tell us about the most efficient, fastest way of doing things so we can save time and money
- We are also into the latest quirky, unique, original or pioneering technology. So long as the system is clever, it doesn't have to be practical. We know there will be an application. It's just a matter of time.

If you stick to the facts, are intelligent and what you say makes sense to us and we are interested, then we will listen, understand and accept what you say.

3. How To Teach Us So We Learn Effectively From You

We learn best by thinking through ideas and by using systems, computer programs and search engines. We are great self-learners and can quickly search blogs, manuals or instructions to immediately apply data to a problem so we can find the most effective solutions.

If a teacher is not factual, efficient or intelligent, then we find ourselves frustrated and bored. We will not tolerate being told what to do by someone who knows less than we do. If you don't know something, let us work it out for ourselves and we will be happy but don't pretend to know something when you don't.

We don't mind if you don't know stuff – we get that you can't know everything – so long as you let us be free to find out for ourselves. Nothing annoys us more than having to do something the accepted way when we know a system that is faster and better. We are not obviously disruptive but when we feel bored or controlled, we are not above being a maverick and creating pranks, hacks or distractions that no one realises are ours.

4. What We Are Like In Relationships

In relationships, one way we tell people we like them is by sharing information or new technology with them. Sometimes partners complain that we are not affectionate or caring enough and that might be because we spend a lot of time in our heads. If someone can keep up with our ideas and keep it real and logical, then we appreciate their practicality and like to hang out with them.

If we are creating something new or have our head in html or a program, then please don't distract us. We will be thinking of what we are doing and won't have the headspace to think of anything else. If you need a lot of attention and affection, you might like to look for someone from another tribe but if you also like ideas, are busy with a project or are a genius, we will give you the space you need. Being with a partner is like a break for us. We enjoy it but then it's back to work.

5. Different Types of Members of Our Tribe

Our tribe is divided into two types, 'Detailers' and 'Abstractors', and some people are both.

Detailers like detail, facts and figures. They like others to be accurate, logical and credible. People sometimes comment that they are not empathic but this heightened intelligence can make them mathematically and technologically gifted.

Abstractors like abstract concepts, philosophy and inventions. Think of Albert Einstein or Socrates. People sometimes comment that these people are distracted or impossible to understand but some of our greatest scientific and philosophical breakthroughs have come from these great minds.

6. How to Enhance Your Audio-Digital Skills and Talents

Make a vow to spend a day totally focused on digital information, lists and details.

Audio-Digital Exercise 1 – Getting Your Head Around Analysis

Think about a mobile phone that you would like to buy. Examine the features of the phone on Google. Compare those features to another phone that is similar. Compare the price to the features. Check out some blogs on the subject. Think about what you want to use the phone for. Analyse which is the best phone for you in terms of value for money. Think about someone else you know who uses a phone for a different purpose than what you do. Analyse which would be the best phone for them. If you see any jargon you don't understand, make sure you check out the meaning and memorise it. Keep a little list on your computer of jargon and their meanings so you can look it up quickly.

Now research the best plan. Analyse the types of calls you make and then figure out which is going to be the best plan for you. Talk to someone who knows a lot about phones and plans and ask them specific questions about features. It takes some getting your head around to begin with, and at first it can seem overwhelming, but after a while you will be surprised at how quickly you can actually learn this kind of information if you pay attention. You will also find that it makes you feel really smart and sound impressive when you can rattle off just a bit of jargon!

The best bit, however, is that you make a great decision which will save you time and money in the long run.

Audio-Digital Exercise 2 – Getting Your Head Around Calculations

This is a great exercise if you don't find it easy to get your head around analysis. Imagine looking at the beach. See the yellow sand and the blue water. Really see the different colours of the water – turquoise, dark blue – and then the bright blue of the sky above it. Look at the children playing on the beach. One little boy has red Hawaiian boardshorts on and another little girl is wearing a pink hat. The children are chasing seagulls around.

You can hear the seagulls squawking and the children laughing and squealing. You can also hear some people talking closer to you and the gentle crash of the waves in the background.

Now think about how long it took you to get to the beach. How many minutes did it take you. Calculate that it took you about 30 minutes at an average of 60 kilometres per hour to get to the beach. If you drove at 30 kilometres per hour, it would have taken you an hour. If you had driven at 90 kilometres per hour, it would have taken you 20 minutes. Did you use the right route? Maybe there was a longer route but because you could go faster on that route it would take you less time. Think about how you would like to check that out on Google Maps when you get home.

What is interesting is that when we are at the beach, the last paragraph might be all we are thinking about. We are not really looking at the view at all!

So it is good to work out what is the best style to use to enjoy different experiences.

Audio-Digital Exercise 3 – Using Logic to Analyse People

Ask someone's opinion about something you are interested in or get them to discuss a problem they may be having with someone else. Analyse what they say. Does it make sense? Think of what they are saying in terms of cause and effect. If they are discussing the way someone has treated them, see if you can work out why someone has treated them in that manner. Does the cause start with the person you are listening to or the person they are talking about? Is the person's reaction logical or emotional? If it's emotional, why would they feel that in this situation? Ask them questions to see if you can analyse what might be causing their reaction. Does this event remind them of something in the past that is triggering a response that is greater than what is warranted?

What conclusions or generalisations is the person making about the situation? Are they logical? Is the initial premise logical? For instance, if someone's boyfriend doesn't return calls and she believes it is because she didn't go to the movies with him on Saturday night, is that a logical conclusion? What do you know about her boyfriend? Would not going to the movies with him that night offend him or not? What other explanations might there be?

Use your knowledge of communication tribes to work out which communication tribe your friend belongs to. What is her dominant and secondary tribe? What is her boyfriend's dominant and secondary tribe? Predict some of the problems they may encounter with communication. Discuss these with your friend and ask her whether your predictions are accurate or not.

What do you think? Analysis can be fun, can't it! Of course if you want to be really Audio-Digital, you can always do your taxes or work out a budget but for most people, analysing others is more interesting and it is still practicing analytical skills.

CONCLUSION

Well we certainly hope that you have found understanding the communication tribes informative, entertaining and fun! Please feel free to visit our web page www.pipmckay.com.au/4tribes1earth and leave a comment as we would love to get your feedback. Please feel free to pass the quiz onto others.

Please remember that communication tribes are not about boxing people but rather as a way of understanding others and ourselves more deeply.

SECTION 3

Understanding the Theory Behind Communication Styles and How the Tribes Came About

BY JENNY AND ANDREW

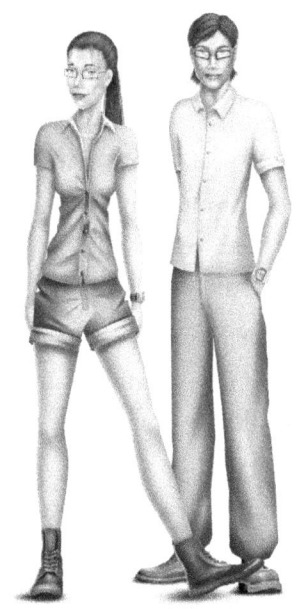

Andrew: Hi, I'm Andrew

Jenny: And I'm Jenny

Andrew: We belong to the Tribe-that-Thinks-and-Calculates. So we thought we would introduce you to the theory side of *4 Tribes 1 Earth*, since everyone else is off involved in either doing some activity, painting pictures or playing music. Most of them felt the story *4 Tribes 1 Earth – A Parable of Communication and Love* was enough but we know there are those out there, like us, who might like the facts in a more information-style format, even though we totally think the story is the best.

Jenny: Yep, we sure do. But maybe that's just because we're in it!

Andrew: Hmm, anyway, the story gives you a great idea of what the different tribes are like, how they interact and how people can adjust their style to communicate effectively with any tribe.

Jenny: So, it's up to us to do the more techo things like describe theory. I hope the word 'theory' doesn't put you off. We'll do our best to make it as interesting as possible.

Andrew: The way we see it is that when we understand our own and other's communication style we will learn more effectively, enhance our ability to communicate and teach, as well as minimise conflict and misunderstandings.

Jenny: From our research we find that most conflict is not a disagreement about information but a mismatch in the way that information is being communicated. But you don't need research to tell you that. I mean how often do two people who love each other end up arguing about silly things? Or after the argument has finished, realise that there are more similarities than differences in what they wanted?

Andrew: Exactly. We know it may sound like a bit of a cliché but we really believe if everyone could spend some more time understanding each other's point of view our world would be a much happier place and children would feel less alone and more cherished.

Jenny: Yeah, people talk about more understanding but most people simply don't have the tools to take their understanding to the next level and that is where the communication tribes are such a vital tool.

Andrew: So feel free to pass it on to your friends and colleagues, especially since the quiz is free!

Jenny: I see – so now we are doing a plug for the quiz, are we?

Andrew: Well it's true.

Jenny: Anyway, it is true. We just feel so strongly that it is vital to ensure that every human being, and particularly every child, has the greatest opportunity to succeed no matter which tribe they come from. We don't have to wait for world peace or something grandiose like that to make a difference. Understanding each other and practicing tolerance can happen every day, in every little interaction with friends, family and anyone we meet.

Andrew: Look we get it; it's not always easy even with people from the same tribe but it is so worth the effort.

Jenny: Yeah, we work with it every day, particularly when stressed or tired. It's easy to be nice when you're happy and life is going well. It's at challenging times that it's important to put in the effort to see things from a different point of view, otherwise you can be triggered by what you think is insensitivity but might just be another way of processing information. In the end, communication is the key.

Andrew: Yeah, making sure it doesn't bottle up and instead, talking it out respectfully. Understanding someone else's point of view while still expressing your own. That's the most important thing.

Jenny: That's right, most people are either doing one or the other. Like they are either good at understanding other people but aren't getting their own needs met or they are getting their own needs met but not understanding other people.

Andrew: The biggest lesson we learnt from the tribes is being able to do both. They are both important otherwise you're not really communicating.

Jenny: Yeah exactly, after all the 'co' in communication means two or more people doing it together. It is the way you create any form of community or cooperation.

Andrew: And on a more work-based level, communication is vital for effective leadership, teamwork and management as well as customer service and sales.

Effective communication reduces stress and increases happiness. For those into facts and figures that means more staff retention, less sick days and bullying, and therefore greater productivity. That makes our whole culture, not just corporate culture, richer and more sophisticated.

Jenny: If you think about it, how much dissatisfaction at home, school or work comes from unhealthy interactions with someone else? Think about the amount of emotional energy, headspace and stress that takes. Imagine what we could achieve if our relationships in all areas of our lives were more effective, supportive and positive?

How good would it be if people knew how to respectfully assert themselves as well as understand others?

Andrew: So let's get started.

Jenny: Great idea! So Andrew will take you through the general theory. Have fun learning!

Andrew: Exactly. Who says you can't have fun and learn at the same time?

General Introduction To Communication Styles – Andrew

As human beings we gather information from the world through our five senses. That's what we touch, see, hear, smell and taste. For most people they take more notice of what they touch, see and hear than what they smell and taste. Then there are our internal senses: so the emotions we feel, the pictures we imagine or remember, our self-talk or replaying conversations with others and finally, abstract thinking, processing numbers and other calculations.

Of course, anyone can use any of their senses at any point in time and we all use all of our senses all of the time, unless we have some kind of disability. However, most people have a habit of being consciously aware of one or two senses most of the time. This habitual approach to our environment, information and way of thinking creates a particular trait in an individual.

It's a bit like the fact that a scientist who is at work is going to have a habit of thinking that is maybe different from an athlete, which may be different from an artist or a musician. It doesn't mean that she can't do sport or paint or play music. It's just that it's not the way she spends most of her time, and the way she spends her time will affect the types of things she thinks about and the types of things she notices. In the end we could do all of them – after all Albert Einstein played the violin! – but most people are only going to have time to master one or two things and this will affect the way they see the world and their personality.

It's the same with the Tribes – each Tribe has an habitual sense they are most consistently aware of and this affects the way they see the world, think, speak and learn, and the development of their culture. Of course, they have access to all of their senses and modes of thinking – this is what they have in common – however their habit of thinking and sensing is what makes them different and individual, and helps them to develop unique gifts.

The character in the story *4 Tribes 1 Earth*, Javier, has equal access to all of his senses and finds it easy to adjust his communication and learning style. This doesn't make him better than anyone else – he just has a habit of using a range of senses which has its own strengths and weaknesses. Someone who has a strong habit in just one particular sense will simply develop a greater depth of experience of that way of being in the world which also will have its own strengths and weaknesses. That's why it is wonderful to open ourselves up to understanding rather than judging others. That way we can easily enrich our experience of the world by seeing it from their point of view.

Personally before I understood the communication tribes, I spent most of my time in my head with abstract thinking and calculations. The information I sought in my world was facts and figures and I would get those mainly by reading.

Now you may say: "Well, you read by seeing and you can get information by hearing a lecture." That's true. Just because I belong to the Tribe-that-Thinks-and-Calculates doesn't mean I can't use all of my senses. I can. It's just that I used to spend most of my time in my head thinking about concepts like: Is it possible to find a pattern in the weather or is it truly random? What equation best describes the data we have gathered about rainfall? I'm sure you get the idea.

I have a friend at uni. He's also from my tribe but he's more interested in philosophy, than calculations. So he spends his time thinking about what it means to be a human being and is there such a thing as absolute truth? Or is it only relative?

So it's not the content of information that makes someone part of my tribe. It's that we are interested in concepts rather than feelings, imaginings or listening. Now please don't get me wrong; all of this has nothing to do with intelligence. I have another friend at uni and she is doing visual arts and art history. So guess which sense she favours? That's right. Of course it's visual. So she would be a part of the Tribe-that-Sees-and-has-Visions even though she lives in the city and goes to uni.

What about this one? This friend was also at uni with me. He studied Drama and English Literature. It's not so easy to tell, is it? He could be interested most in listening to the language and therefore be a part of the Tribe-that-Listens-and-Sings, but he's not. He's part of the Tribe-that-Moves-and-is-Touched. He is always up acting out the scenes in plays and getting in touch with the emotions of the characters.

So in the end, even though many tribes are attracted to subjects that reflect their style, it's not always that easy to guess. It is a good starting point however if you really want to guess someone else's style think about what type of information or experience someone is searching for. If you are interested in Shakespeare because of the rhythm of the language, then it's more likely to be auditory information you are listening for. That's like the Tribe-that-Listens-and-Sings. If you are interested in Shakespeare because you love the action or the emotions of the characters, then it is more likely you are interested in kinesthetic information. That's the Tribe-that-Moves-and-is-Touched. Kinesthetic just means movement that could be physical action or being moved emotionally. So people who are most attracted to this type of information belong to the Tribe-that-Moves-and-is-Touched.

In the end, communication tribes are not about boxing yourself or others. It's about identifying tendencies, patterns and habits of speech and how this affects the way you see the world, interact with others, communicate and learn. It's about understanding yourself and others at a deeper level and being able to more easily see where someone else is coming from and why they think and behave in the way that they do.

We also find, like many of the characters in the book, that people often have two favoured communication styles, although one is usually dominant. So you may find yourself with characteristics of a couple of different tribes. Of course you can also adopt the point of view of another tribe, even one that uses a sense you are not used to, and this can enrich your experience of the world and expand your horizons. When you learn to adjust to the way others experience the world, you can see the same scene from four completely different perspectives and each will give you a new experience and way of seeing. This also assists problem solving and inclusion of different points of view for team engagement.

Why Are the Tribes Different?

The Tribes grew up separately in isolated areas of the earth. They developed their own unique culture based on the SENSE they most favoured and the nature of their environment. This created their communication tribe and learning tendencies.

The Tribe-that-Sees-and-has-Visions

The Tribe-that-Sees-and-has-Visions grew up in the Painted Desert. They had wandered the earth looking for a safe place to settle away from the Eye-of-Envy that had killed so many of their number. When they found the inhospitable but beautiful Painted Desert, they stopped there, knowing that this at last was a place where they could belong and rear their children in peace.

To sustain themselves through their long journey they had to be crystal clear about their vision. Focusing on sight also allowed them to stay out of the despairing emotions that threatened to overwhelm them. The sense of sight became their hope, their refuge and their entire point of view and this is the sense they still favour today.

The Tribe-that-Moves-and-is-Touched

The Tribe-that-Moves-and-is-Touched grew up in the Forest of Rain. They have been there since time began and their roots grow deep into the earth that sustains them. The forest was a nurturing and generous mother, gentle and soft with rainfall. The Tribe grew up happy and passionate. It was safe for them to express and feel deep emotions. They were also physically robust because of the abundance of food in the forest.

The more deeply they plunged into their emotions and felt their physical body, the more of the earth they could experience and the stronger they became. The sense of touch became their altar, their passion and their entire way of being and this is still the sense they favour today.

The Tribe-that-Listens-and-Sings

The Tribe-that-Listens-and–Sings grew up in Echo Canyon. Legend has it that they were sung into being by a Great Bird whose song echoed in the canyon until sound became form. The river that runs through the centre of the canyon is filled with minerals from the canyon walls. As a result, thousands of birds flock to the river and pools, as well as frogs, insects and other wildlife creating a cacophony of nature sounds.

Harmonising, talking, listening, storytelling and singing became a natural part of everyday life, as the tribe found their place among the sounds of nature. The sense of hearing became their muse, their inspiration and their total immersion and this is still the sense they favour today.

The Tribe-that-Thinks-and-Calculates

The Tribe-that-Thinks-and-Calculates grew up in the City of Concrete. Originally all the members of the city came from the other three tribes, but as this tribe became more removed from nature, they took less notice of their external senses and went more and more into their heads.

Thought, calculations, digital information, gadgets and information technology became what occupied all of their time. Even connecting with others of their tribe was filtered through electronic devices and programs. Thinking, facts and figures became their preoccupation and infatuation and it is still the way of processing information that they favour today.

SPOILER ALERT!

WHERE DID THE IDEA OF COMMUNICATION STYLES COME FROM?

Warning! Do not read this if you want to stay in the world created by *4 Tribes 1 Earth*. (Of course you can always read it and then re-immerse yourself in the tribes. This section takes away a bit of the fantasy however I believe in recognising my academic sources).

In the 1970s, Richard Bandler and John Grinder were interested in the study of how we know what we know or epistemology. They looked at the way people take in information from their world, how they process it internally and filter it according to their beliefs, values and experiences, and then how that affects their thinking and behaviour.

They called their study 'NLP' or Neuro-Linguistic Programming. They also spent a great deal of time modelling and understanding three of the most effective psychotherapists of their time who were very different from each other and had very different approaches. From this study they were able to create a unique approach to understanding human behaviour that unified seemingly contrasting ways of working to effect change. They modelled Fritz Pearls, the founder of Gestalt therapy, Virginia Satir, a well known family therapist and Dr Milton Erickson, a psychiatrist and hypnotherapist.

Among many of the discoveries of NLP were representational systems or the way we make internal representations of memory or imagination. How do we represent our experiences and our environment in our mind and how do we rearrange representations to create new thoughts? What they found was that our internal representations mirror our senses. We can represent something as a vision – seeing, soundtrack – hearing, emotion or movement

– kinesthetic, taste – gustatory or smell – olfactory. There was one more internal representation, which does not necessarily correlate to a sense, and that is abstract thinking – concepts or calculations. This type of thinking they labelled audio-digital. NLP categorised the dominant internal representations as Visual, Auditory, Kinesthetic and Audio-Digital.

The founders of NLP worked out that there were two ways the representational systems worked: one was the preferred system which was the one most frequently or noticeably used to express yourself. The other was the lead system which was an internal system that leads you to using other representations. For instance, someone might imagine something and then have a feeling about it like excitement. Someone else might feel something first, like happiness, and then have some self-talk about what they just felt, like: "Oh I wonder why I feel happy? Must be the weather".

The founders of NLP have gone to great lengths to ensure that people do not think of themselves as visual people or kinesthetic people etc and box themselves and others in this way. They felt that these labels limit the variety of processing someone can experience and might not describe the reality of their experience. One of the cornerstones of NLP is the idea of curiosity, so instead of presuming you know someone, really observe them carefully and ask about their experience. It is possible that labels can interfere with that process because people tend to gain closure and a sense of knowing before they have really explored someone else's model of the world.

So in some ways, categorising the representational systems into tribes has the possibility of going against the original intention of the founders of NLP.

Pip McKay, however, felt that the different habits of communication do create strong preferences in both communication and learning which, if easily described and codified, could then be a very useful shorthand for people in relationships, sales, management and in particular, teachers and parents. Pip is passionate about the need to cater for all children's learning styles so that children can learn effectively in a way that suits them and fulfils their potential.

As a result, she created *4 Tribes 1 Earth* for three main purposes:

1. As a way of understanding ourselves and others better
2. Fostering effective communication, and

3. Gathering data that might encourage educational institutions to incorporate a wider variety of communication styles in teaching so that more children can feel confident in their capacity to learn and be understood.

Too many children have challenges learning in school, not because of intelligence or capacity, but because the learning environment is still geared towards the minority of students who have an auditory and audio-digital learning style. In a way, it is a form of hidden discrimination. The communication tribes allows us to see the differences and cater for a greater number of children and adults to enhance experience, learning and understanding. By embracing differences we enhance peace and harmony and help a greater number of people fulfil their potential.

PIP McKAY'S LEARNING JOURNEY

Pip is a pioneer within the field of personal development and coaching. She is the author of *4 Tribes 1 Earth* and *The 8 Principles of Achievement, Love & Happiness* as well as numerous CD and DVD resources and live courses. At school Pip was dyslexic and favoured a kinesthetic and visual approach to learning. In year 9, while required to do two hours of prep, supervised homework at boarding school, she discovered the way she processed information. She realised that if she could get a clear picture of something or connect emotionally to the teacher, the story or the feeling captured inside the information, then she could learn and remember it. From then on her marks went up by 40% and she went from being an average student to exceptional.

She was then able to go to university where she studied English Literature and gained a BA Honours degree. She still had problems with spelling and her reading rate was slow, however she found that these issues were more than compensated for by her ability to have unique insights that others missed and by her heightened sense of creativity. She went on to do a Diploma of Education at The University of Sydney, was Dux of her year and won the PR Cole Memorial Prize for excellence. Pip took her unique way of seeing things and her special ability to empathise and understand others into the classroom where she was an outstanding teacher. She was chosen to be a GCSE examiner of English in the United Kingdom and HSC examiner of Drama in Australia.

After leaving teaching, Pip studied NLP and set up her own successful training organization called *Evolve Now Mind Institute Pty Ltd*. She then created *Matrix Therapies*®, *Archetypal Coaching*® and *Passion and Purpose Coaching* personal development and coaching tools. These help people make profound emotional change and *Kids Matrix*® which assists parents and teachers to help children learn and grow. Pip then created *4 Tribes 1 Earth* as a simple way for adults, parents, teachers and children to understand more easily how to communicate with each other and learn more effectively.

Pip's first published book, *The 8 Principles of Success, Love and Happiness* was an Amazon No.1 bestseller in Australia, UK, USA and Canada and won the prestigious EIPPY Award in Los Angeles.

If you would like more information about Pip McKay, visit www.pipmckay.com.au. *Matrix Therapies*® and *Kid's Matrix*® are available on CD and DVD in the online shop and many of Pip's courses are listed on her website.

Remember the website for the quiz is: www.pipmckay.com.au/4tribes1earth

Reading Pip's books is transformational, attending a course is life-changing. We look forward to meeting you and hearing how this work makes a difference to your life.